Cindy Lora-Renard

Foreword by Gary R. Renard

A COURSE
IN
HEALTH
AND
WELL-BEING

From Principles Of
A COURSE IN MIRACLES

"This book is a shining gem. I want to use the word practical to describe it but that seems a bit ordinary for a book that is anything but. And yet, much of the words you'll read will have a practical impact on your life, which is what any author hopes to accomplish. Cindy shows how her own choices led her to listen deeply to the Holy Spirit, and she shows how we can all do the same thing. I've known Cindy and have heard her share her wisdom before, and I'm so happy she's stepping out into the light. Her voice is clear and radiant."

— **James Twyman, NY Times Bestselling author of The Moses Code and The Barn Dance**

"Cindy Lora-Renard gets to the heart of the miracle of healing with her new book. It sparkles with the simple clarity, certainty, and compassion that only an expression of truth can offer. I know this, having returned from death five times after experiencing that miracle; and it *does* take miracles to awaken us to our real health. Cindy's book is not only about the true nature of healing, reading it will help to heal you. Applying the wisdom she offers in this book in your daily life will help free you. It's a delightful read-and profound. You'll learn to see more clearly and love more dearly."

— **Michael J. Tamura, Spiritual Teacher, Clairvoyant Visionary, Healing Pioneer, and Author of YOU ARE THE ANSWER: Discovering and Fulfilling Your Soul's Purpose**

"A beautiful companion to A Course in Miracles! This inspiring book offers you a *holy shift* from ego to soul, lack to abundance, suffering to forgiveness, conflict to peace, and fear to love."

— **Robert Holden, author of Holy Shift: 365 Meditations from A Course in Miracles**

Cindy Lora-Renard

Foreword by Gary R. Renard

A COURSE
IN
HEALTH
AND
WELL-BEING

Copyright, 2017

by

Cindy Lora-Renard

All quotes from *A Course in Miracles*© are from the
Third Edition, 2007.

Used with permission from the copyright holder and publisher,
the Foundation for Inner Peace, P.O. Box 598,
Mill Valley, CA 94942-0598.

www.acim.org and info@acim.org.

For my brother, Jeff Ray

We are One forever

We have nothing to do, but everything to be.

Cindy Lora-Renard

CONTENTS

ACKNOWLEDGMENTS

I am deeply grateful to my husband, Gary Renard, for being willing to share the teachings of *A Course in Miracles* in all of his books, as well as for his constant support of my own path with the *Course*. He has encouraged me to follow through on all of my personal projects as well as the projects we do together. His loving and generous attitude is noted and appreciated. We have experienced a lot together as a couple, and every experience has been a blessing to me as we awaken in God together.

I would also like to acknowledge and thank my beautiful mother, Doris Lora, who has contributed her editing skills to this project. She has also remained a consistent model and demonstration of the teachings of *A Course in Miracles*. Her endless encouragement and support of my path is deeply appreciated.

I am forever grateful to my dear sister, Jackie Lora Jones, who walks this spiritual path with me. Her endless love and inspiration goes with me wherever I go. I am blessed to have her consistent presence in my life.

My sincere gratitude to my father, Ron Lora, for always supporting me in everything I do for as long as I remember. His authentic curiosity with all the happenings in my life is very meaningful to me, and I am deeply grateful.

I would like to acknowledge the late, great Dr. Kenneth Wapnick, the most prolific writer in his work with *A Course in Miracles* who really understood the teachings of Jesus. I have received much inspiration in my study and practice of the *Course* from both him and his lovely wife, Gloria Wapnick, founders of the Foundation for *A Course in Miracles* in Temecula, CA.

My deepest gratitude goes to the authorized publisher and copyright holder of *A Course in Miracles*, the Foundation for Inner Peace, for their years of dedication in making the *Course* available to millions of people around the world.

Finally, I sincerely thank all of my family and friends who have profoundly influenced my life in positive ways. I thank them for always loving, encouraging, and inspiring me to walk confidently on my chosen path. Their support has great meaning for me, and I am blessed to have them in my life.

FOREWORD

At first I was hesitant to write this Foreword, Cindy being my wife. I thought people might think I'm biased. Actually I am, but not in the way you might assume. I'm biased in favor of *A Course in Miracles*, as well as my four books that teach it. I refuse to compromise on its relentlessly non-dualistic teachings. One of the interesting things about Cindy's book is that, just as in the occasional workshops we lead together, Cindy also refuses to compromise on the *Course*. In fact, if she did compromise on it I wouldn't be able to work with her.

Over the last ten years, it's been a genuine pleasure for me to watch Cindy develop into a world class spiritual teacher; from coming to my workshops and not saying anything, to providing music, to speaking at first for short periods of time, to longer talks, Cindy has steadily improved every year to the point where I'd put her up there with the best of the best.

On the level of this dream, Cindy comes from a very strong gene pool. Her father is an award winning history professor, and her mom has two Ph.D's, one in psychology and the other in music. It's no surprise that Cindy's main interests are psychology and music. Cindy received her Master's Degree in Spiritual Psychology from the University of Santa Monica, which was one of the few places in the world that offered a degree in spiritual psychology. She's smarter than me, but I forgive her.

I've never seen anyone read the *Course* as much as Cindy. This was always the case, from the time we moved in together to the time we got married eight years ago, to today. The *Course* is her passion (aside from me, I hope.) She talks so much about it that once in a while I have to say, "Cindy, please. Give me a break! Can we play normal for a while?"

This is a book about healing, and Cindy knows what she's talking about. She understands that all sickness is of the mind, and that all healing is of the mind. It's the Holy Spirit who actually does the healing, but if you can change your perception to be in line with that of the Holy Spirit, this allows the Holy Spirit to do the job. As the *Course* puts it, mind is "the activating agent of spirit, supplying its creative energy.[1]" This book, like *A Course in Miracles*, is about changing your mind, which is cause, knowing that in turn, the effect will take care of itself. It couldn't be any other way. To paraphrase Shakespeare, "…it must follow, as the night the day…"

Cindy sticks to the *Course's* non-dualistic philosophy. To the uninitiated, that means the *Course* is saying that of the two seeming worlds, the world of God and the world of humans, only the world of God is true, and nothing else is true. As my Teachers, Arten and Pursah, have taught me, there are two words that express the absolute truth: God Is. I think it's fairly easy for students to accept that God Is. What's hard for them to get is that nothing else is. Cindy doesn't deviate from the absolute truth, but at the same time she doesn't deny that our experience is that we are here; that we have seemingly real problems, bills to pay, jobs to do and relationships to try and make work. It's not the purpose of this book to deny those experiences, but it is the purpose of this book to point out that they are false experiences. What we are seeing is not true, because this is a dream we will awaken from, and it's that awakening that is enlightenment.

You'll find great knowledge in this book, from the real purpose of the body, to dealing with pain, which is the product of unconscious guilt. You will also learn that experiencing mental health always comes back to the power of choice. *A Course in Miracles* teaches that the power of decision is your only true power in this world, and Cindy explains how to use that power. Throughout it all, she has a knack for expressing the

Course in a language that everyone can accept and understand. The ability she has shown to articulate advanced spiritual principles in our workshops shines through in these pages. I encourage you to enjoy the book, and also to learn from it. The right part of your mind, the part where the Holy Spirit dwells, will thank you.

Gary R. Renard, July 2017

CHAPTER 1

INTRODUCTION

When the ego tempts you to sickness do not ask the Holy Spirit to heal the body, for this would merely be to accept the ego's belief that the body is the proper aim of healing. Ask, rather, that the Holy Spirit teach you the right perception *of the body, for perception alone can be distorted. Only perception can be sick, because only perception can be wrong.*[1]

This is the first book in a three-part series. The series expands on various themes from the modern non-dualistic spiritual masterpiece, *A Course in Miracles*. The themes I choose to address for this first book shed light on some of the most commonly asked questions that I receive at the workshops on *A Course in Miracles* I do with my husband, author Gary R. Renard. Specifically,

I discuss *the Course's* approach in the areas of health and well-being, both at the mental and physical levels. As we go along, you'll see that everything we experience is a mental process, not a physical one. This is not your typical health book that defines health only in terms of the body being well. That would be too limiting. The body is not the source of its own health, because it's the mind that decides to be well. This choice can be reflected in the body being healed or appearing well. *A Course in Miracles* teaches that we are not bodies, although that certainly seems to be our experience. What we really are is perfect spirit. In a purely non-dualistic thought system, this means that if you believe in *both* a world of God and of man, that is dualism. Only one of these is true - the Kingdom of God, which is perfect oneness. Perfect oneness never shifts or changes or takes on form, so that means that anything that can shift or change or take on form is an illusion (a dream). This includes all of our dream lifetimes. When I specifically refer to another lifetime of mine in this book, it is for the purpose of showing how it can be used to deepen the awareness that we are eternal beings. It also explains why we are drawn to certain ideas, people and situations as you will see in my story below. Most of us believe we are bodies living in a physical world, so *A Course in Miracles* speaks to us where we believe we are, but it is really addressing all of us as one mind.

I am well aware that practicing non-dualism can seem pretty intense at times, because it implies that not only is there no world, but the "you" who you think you are (the personality) is not real either. Therefore, this requires us to question everything we've been taught thus far about our identity. I have found that it's helpful to not take myself too seriously, and remember to laugh. I, personally, take my awakening seriously, but not the world itself, which is a projection of the ego. It is utterly unbelievable, and therefore not worth lamenting about. However, one can be "normal" and have compassion for self and others in the dream (the world) without being attached to it. When you realize you are dreaming, the goal is to awaken from the dream.

From this point on, when I refer to *A Course in Miracles*, I will simply say the *Course*. Most of the material that will be discussed in this book takes its inspiration from the *Course*. It is important to note that the Voice of the *Course* itself is Jesus. The Course was channeled through a woman named Helen Schucman in the 60's, who heard His voice very clearly and wrote down everything He said. In the references section in the back of this book, I will include a selection of titles that I believe will help further your understanding of the *Course*. In addition, all of the quotes I use in this book will be footnoted and these are listed as Endnotes also in the back of the book.

The *Course* itself explains, in the Preface, how it came into being, what it is, and what it says. Although I will be discussing the *Course's* thought system as we go along, I highly recommend reading the *Course* itself. It's a mind-opener! In the *Course,* Jesus and the Holy Spirit are the same thing, since Jesus had become totally identified with the Christ in his final lifetime as Jesus, so he is now a symbol of the Holy Spirit and represents Its thought system of love, innocence, and wholeness. So when I refer to Jesus in this book, it can also be taken to mean the Holy Spirit. Also, whenever I am referring to a higher authority such as Jesus, the Holy Spirit, or God, I will capitalize the word or words that are related as I've done above. Although the *Course* uses Christian terminology, please note that it is not a religion, nor was it ever meant to be a religion. It is a self-study thought system that is between you and the Holy Spirit that helps one to undo the ego. The term "ego" is used to stand for the false self, based on the false idea that we have been separated from our Source. Jesus uses Christian terms for a reason, and many of the traditional meanings of certain words used in Christianity are completely re-framed in the *Course* to mean something different. He also uses Freudian concepts (Helen Schucman, the scribe, was a clinical psychologist) especially the defense mechanisms familiar in Western culture and brilliantly discusses their use by the mind. As I use these redefined terms in this book, their meaning will become clear to you.

This book is not meant to replace the *Course* itself, so it should not be used as a substitute. If the *Course* is or becomes your chosen path, I highly recommend reading both the text and doing the workbook, which consists of 365 lessons, one for every day of the year.

The daily workbook lessons aid you in the undoing of the ego and sets you on a right-minded path. Many of us want to end our pain and suffering in all the forms it takes, and here along comes a thought system, a spiritual technology with detailed exercises, that helps us do just that! It gets to the root cause of all suffering, which is guilt, a concept that I will expand on in this book. If the *Course* is your chosen path, it is encouraging you to follow what it says and practice, practice, practice! Doing the workbook is the beginning of learning to practice in a specific way. Once you complete the workbook, the goal is to be as consistent as you can in keeping up with the daily practice of undoing the ego.

I know from experience that it is absolutely necessary to keep these ideas fresh in the mind or else the ego will dominate your thoughts and reinforce fear. The *Course* has changed my life significantly over the years and has helped me move through some very anxious times. I know it's done the same for many people. It's always interesting to hear how other people find the *Course*. I'd like to share with you how I came to the *Course*, including how I met my husband, Gary Renard, a very prominent *Course* teacher. Also, I highly recommend Gary's book trilogy starting with *The Disappearance of the Universe,* followed by *Your Immortal Reality,* and then *Love Has Forgotten No One,* which explains the *Course* very well, and the whole back story of some of the things I will be mentioning in my story. It will then make even more sense to you.

Back in the 90's when I was in my 20's, I started reading lots of spiritual type books, but I was most interested in psychic phenomena, near death experiences, and out of body experiences. I believe my interest in spirituality was influenced by the following: My mother had been on a spiritual search since the 80's when Shirley Maclaine came out with "Out On A Limb," and she was talking quite a bit about the things she was learning from her books, among other sources as well. My mother and I would have many interesting conversations about metaphysical topics, and I had a very open mind at that point. I soaked up the ideas like a sponge! Also, my interest in near death experiences had started when I was even younger in my early teens after I learned that my grandmother had one, and she reported it to my father, explaining the tunnel she went through with a bright light at the end of the tunnel. Then, during the 90's I started to have out-of-body experiences pretty frequently, and found great freedom in exploring the spiritual realms without any bodily limits. It was liberating! This peaked my interest in spiritual matters even more.

During this time, I would go to a local bookstore and always go to the metaphysical section. I would always take *A Course in Miracles* off the shelf and open a few pages of it. I usually ended up putting it right back on the shelf since I had no idea what it was saying. It was like it was in a foreign language. But I could tell it was intelligent writing, and I was intrigued. This went on for several years in my 20's, taking the book off the shelf and putting it back. Then, one day I decided to buy it. I didn't know why since I didn't understand it, but I felt guided to buy it. It ended up sitting on my shelf at home as well for several more years. One day my mother asked me if she could borrow my copy. Soon after that she started attending a study group on *A Course in Miracles* in her area, and ended up sharing the lessons with me, and we would have a discussion about it. I still wasn't inspired to read it yet, but I felt I would at some point. Then, one day my mother called me and told me about a book she took home from her *Course* group called "The Disappearance of the Universe." She was raving about it! She absolutely loved this book, and the author, Gary R. Renard. She mentioned to me how funny Gary was and that his style of writing made the *Course* so much easier to understand. I took a look at the book, and stared at Gary's picture on the back cover. I immediately felt I knew him. I couldn't explain why at the time, but I felt I knew his Soul. Everything about him was familiar to me; his face, smile and sarcastically funny attitude. I found myself staring at his picture quite frequently as if I was trying to place him. I read the book and knew that I found my path. Gary's Ascended Master teachers who appear to him, Arten and Pursah, explained everything in the *Course* with such precision, and incorporated humor, which worked very well. I started reading the *Course* and doing the workbook lessons immediately after I read his book. This was in 2005. I would never look back.

Little did I know that one day I would be married to Gary, speak in public about the *Course*, and end up writing a book about it! If someone had told me this would happen back in the 90's I would have said, "What have you been smoking?" At that time, I was interested in being in the entertainment industry, and I had many jobs in the entertainment field, singing in bands, and I also enjoyed being around animals, something that I still enjoy. But teaching *A Course in Miracles*? I never would have thought that, although psychics would tell me that one day I would be speaking in public and write books. I always thought, "How is that going to happen?" I was really shy.

So, in the early part of 2006, my mother asked me if I wanted to meet her in Las Vegas to hear Gary speak. I had been thinking about attending one of his events earlier that year, but it didn't work out, so when my mother asked me about attending one in Las Vegas in May of that year, it was the perfect time. We went to the event and were waiting for Gary to come up and speak. I looked to my right and saw him walking down the aisle. My mother pointed and said, "Look! There's Gary!" We were very excited! I noticed him walking and I had that feeling again that I really knew him. I even knew his walk and body language like I had seen it before. It was a strange feeling, but nice. After the talk, my mother and I waited in the book signing line to say hello. My mother was ahead of me, so she met Gary first. As soon as my mother started talking to Gary, I could tell immediately that he was trying to place her, like he knew her. That was interesting. They had a nice, short exchange. Then it was my turn. I said hello and told him that I really resonated with his books and the messages. I could see the look on his face, and could tell that he was also trying to place me, like he knew me. Knowing he was a musician, I said to him that I was a musician and that I have a website that I would love for him to check out if he had the time. He was very kind and said he'd love to see it. Our exchange was short, but sweet. I started to say good-bye, and started to walk away. As I was walking away, he said, "Is there a way I can reach you on your website?" I said yes. About 3 days later, I received an email from Gary saying that when he met me he felt he knew me. He said I brought back memories for him from other lifetimes, and he asked me if I'd be interested in exploring this more. I absolutely felt the same way, and we kept in touch, which led to him moving out to California to live with me in 2007. We got married in 2009.

It wasn't until later that summer of 2006 when I read his second book, "Your Immortal Reality," that I came to the realization that Arten, one of Gary's Ascended Master teachers in his books, who was also one of Jesus's disciples, Thaddeus, was my future self, now appearing to Gary. I had already learned from his books that Pursah, the female Ascended Master was Jesus's Disciple, Thomas, which was Gary in this lifetime. So, needless to say, it all fit together that we would meet again as Gary and Cindy, and continue to spread the messages of Jesus. It happened one day as I was sitting in my car and was reading a chapter in his book called "Who's Arten?" In this chapter, Arten and Pursah talk with Gary about how he is going to meet Arten in this lifetime and she is a woman. When I read it, it was as if I had heard the conversations before, and I knew they were talking about me. It was like an "Aha" moment. I was filled with wonder and it was a very fascinating experience for me. I didn't say anything to Gary at first because I wanted to wait until he said something. But a couple months after that we were having dinner together, and I started to bring it up. He was very receptive to having the conversation, and he admitted that he knew at the very beginning when he first met me in the book signing line that he had found me. It became very clear to me in that moment, which I'll never forget, that my life was about to do a 180. Everything started to make sense; all the dreams I had up to that point about being with Jesus 2000 years ago, and feeling close to him, as well as my spiritual path up to that point, which was clearly preparing me for what was to come. It became clear to both Gary and me that we were meant to meet, and that we had work to do together, to continue spreading the true teachings of Jesus that he taught 2000 years ago, which was a non-dualistic thought system, using Love and Forgiveness to help lead us home. That thought system continues through His teachings in *A Course in Miracles*. I am honored to now be a part of this path, and absolutely delighted to share these teachings with you, as it reinforces them in my own mind, and keeps me on the path to awakening to the home I never left in

God. Telling my story to you of how I found the *Course* and met Gary, as well as my passion for these teachings, will help you to understand things I may write about in future books as well.

I was also blessed to have received my Master's Degree in Spiritual Psychology from the University of Santa Monica in 2009. My Spiritual Psychology Professors, Dr.'s Ron & Mary Hulnick, truly understand that nothing outside of you is the cause of your upset (a common theme in the *Course*) and I am grateful that they are still offering their services at this wonderful institution of learning. I have often felt that what they are teaching is a very nice compliment to the *Course's* teachings, especially in the areas of forgiveness and their understanding of projection, among many other helpful, psychological tools they offer in service to growth and well-being. Anyone interested in pursuing certification in life coaching using practical, spiritually based psychological methods would, in my opinion, benefit from taking such a course at USM.

A lot of the questions that Gary and I receive at our workshops are in the areas of health and well-being, thus the focus of this book. Therefore, most of the content will come from the *Course's* perspective on how one can look at the various situations regarding the body and our relationships, and our resulting mental and emotional reactions.

I will be referring to passages and ideas in both the *Course* and in Gary's books, as all of the information is connected. I can't help but also be influenced by the great, late teacher of the *Course*, Dr. Kenneth Wapnick. He was there at the beginning with Dr. Helen Schucman, Bill Thetford (co-scribe of the Course and Helen's colleague) and Judy Skutch Whitson, the publisher of the *Course*. I think Dr. Wapnick understood the teachings of the *Course* better than anyone except for Helen herself and wrote many books and pamphlets expounding on its teachings. Therefore I have also studied his writings and highly recommend them. So, I can't help but be influenced by him as well.

For anyone who might be new to the *Course*, I want to reiterate that it is a purely non-dualistic thought system. This means you recognize God as the only reality. Nothing else exists. In order for a lot of the ideas I will be discussing in this book to make sense, it will be helpful if it is read within this context. The *Course* itself is designed to help us undo the ego, which is the false self-concept we made up, based on separation, which has nothing to do with our reality. Reality is God, which is perfect Love. In a non-dualistic system, there is nothing else but God. The introduction to the *Course* states it this way:

"Nothing real can be threatened. Nothing unreal exists. Herein lies the peace of God."[2]

Another way to look at the statement above is to think in terms of Oneness and wholeness. The *Course* says, "Oneness is simply the idea that God is. And in

His being, He encompasses all things. No mind holds anything but Him. We say 'God is,' and then we cease to speak, for in that knowledge words are meaningless. There are no lips to speak them, and no part of mind sufficiently distinct to feel that it is now aware of something not itself. It has united with its Source. And like its Source Itself, it merely is."[3]

In light of the statements above, part of the learning is to accept the Atonement for ourselves, which really means that we recognize that the separation from God never occurred. We are only having a dream of separation. Atonement in the *Course* does not mean the same thing as Atonement in traditional Christianity, that is, atonement for sin. The *Course* says there is no sin, so we don't need to atone for it. Sin is merely the idea of separation. We are only dreaming a dream of separation, and we will wake up from the dream and realize we never left our home in God. Ahh…what a nice thought. Have you ever awakened from a nightmare and said to yourself, "Thank God it was just a dream!" Then you were so relieved that all of the events in the dream weren't real. Well, that is similar to the experience we will all have when all of us awaken from this dream we call the world. We will just experience that it was totally made up and the dream disappears. All of this will become more clear as the ego is undone, and all that will be left is true understanding.

We are result-oriented beings, and this book will attempt to do just that; produce results. If you want to be a master at anything, practice is essential. I do not claim to be a master of these ideas, but I do claim to follow a true master, the Holy Spirit or Jesus as my guide. Jesus and the Holy Spirit represent the right part of our minds, where the Holy Spirit resides; the Holy Spirit is also understood as the great Correction Principle, or Atonement principle that says nothing happened, and the separation from God hasn't occurred. You are still innocent, whole, and perfect in God, which is reality. Since the mind appeared to split after believing we separated from God, it is explained in the Course that we now appear to have a wrong mind (the ego which is based on separation) and a right mind (representing the Holy Spirit, which is based on wholeness, innocence and love). Whichever one we identify with at any given moment is what we believe we are. **We believe what we want to believe, and therefore, we see what we want to see.**

The ideas in this book, along with the suggested exercises, should not be meant to replace any existing treatment or advice from a doctor. This information, which is inspired from the ideas in the Course, is meant to address the level of the mind, where true change occurs, so that the effect can take care of itself. Jesus is encouraging us not to look to effects, but look to the cause instead, which is the choice in our minds for either the Holy Spirit or the ego as our mental guide and teacher. Whichever teacher we choose, our experience will reflect it. I've noticed in my own life how much smoother things go when I choose to let go of my own judgment on things, and let the Holy Spirit take over. The events might not appear to change, but my experience of the event changes, and it is more peaceful. That is worth everything. The *Course* says if you don't like how you feel, you have the power to choose. You are in charge of your mind!

In this book I will also address how taking care of the mind can have positive effects on your state of health, physically, although that is not the goal. It's important to understand that sometimes body issues don't go away even if you attempt to clean out the mind of the ego's "raucous shrieks" that block our real thoughts. That doesn't matter. Ultimately, having a healthy body or a sick body still isn't the Truth, because bodies aren't who we are. The important thing is recognizing that the true goal is that you can be in a state of peace regardless of what is going on with your body, which is really in your mind. The *Course* says, "Ideas leave not their source."[4] So, the world has not left our minds. Everything is in the mind, including your body, which means you can change your mind about it. Cause and effect are not separated, they are One. When I refer to well-being, I will be talking more about the mental state, and how one can experience Divine connection to Spirit; Spirit being that which you really are, one with God. I will be repeating certain ideas as we go along for positive reinforcement.

Although the world is an illusion, it doesn't mean you don't take care of yourself or do things that you feel are naturally healthy for you. You will always have preferences one way or another, and there is nothing wrong with that. Just because water is an illusion doesn't mean you don't drink it. As long as we believe we are bodies, living in a physical world, we need to do the common sense things that help us thrive. The *Course* calls any outside source we use to treat ourselves, "magic." This is simply consistent with the concept that the physical is not true. However, attempting to try and prove that you don't need certain things like food and water, or even medicine because the world and your body are an illusion, won't get you very far. It's always best to just follow the inspired guidance that naturally comes forth within you, which will lead you to the things that will serve you mentally and physically, if it's coming from love.

You are always exactly where you need to be and there are no accidents. Nothing happens at random. Because of the *Course's* focus on mind training, it's more important how you are thinking about things rather than what you are doing. If you are thinking like the Holy Spirit, and practicing right minded thoughts, that is what is important. No matter what appears to be going on, you are always taken care of and in the Light of God. The *Course* says, "You are not a body, you are love, and it matters not where love appears to be, for being love it cannot be wrong."[5] I like to think of this line whenever I am in a challenging situation. It reminds me that no matter what is going on or where I appear to be, when I am thinking with love then I am always at the right place at the right time. When love is in your mind you are also in a better position to hear the Voice of the Holy Spirit and follow Its guidance. You will learn that there is a difference between inspiration that comes from the Holy Spirit, and the guidance of the ego, which are two mutually exclusive states of mind. This will help you discern the difference between the two voices in your mind: One leads to pain and suffering, reinforcing the guilt over the alleged separation from Source (the ego concept), and the other leads to joy and peace, and represents the Holy Spirit. Your mood will always tell you which one you have chosen.

It's also important to understand the causal connection between how you feel and what you are thinking in your mind at any given moment. Herein lies the value of mindfulness. Once you begin to associate how you are feeling with what you've been thinking, you can start to take control of the thoughts you are thinking in your mind and remember you always have a choice in how you interpret anything that is going on. It's the thoughts that come first. Feeling follows thought. We first make an interpretation of someone or something by thinking about it a certain way, and then we experience our thoughts through feelings. The thoughts remain the cause of how we feel, so it is at the mind level where we have true power to change our thinking and interpretations, and thereby changing how we experience things.

Now you may begin to recognize that nothing outside of you is the cause of pain and suffering. This thought alone can set you on the path toward freedom from any suffering you may be experiencing. If it were true that something outside of you could cause you to suffer, you would certainly be a victim of the world. There is no power in that. The *Course* says, "I am not the victim of the world I see."[6] This is because the world is just a projection coming from your mind. There is no world outside of you. You see what you want to see, and that is all. With practice and willingness, you can learn to see right-mindedly, with Truth as your goal, and with Christ Vision, which is true vision, true perception, and innocence.

I invite you to join me on this healing journey with Spirit, and learn to let go of the ego's plan, and invest your faith in what is true and permanent: a plan that never fails; the plan of the Holy Spirit, which will lead you out of suffering, and into your true nature as Spirit; the home you never left.

CHAPTER 2

WHAT IS HEALTH?

*Health is the result of relinquishing all
attempts to use the body lovelessly.*[1]

As I was sitting in the back of the room one day in
Winterthur, Switzerland, listening to my husband's
talk on *A Course in Miracles,* he said "Jesus isn't coming
back because he became enlightened." On the level of
the world, that is a true statement; that Jesus was once
a man in a body who became the Christ, which all of
us will awaken to as well. When you are enlightened
there is no need to return in body form. In reality, none
of us are really in a body, as the body is a projection
coming from the mind. After that statement that Gary
made, my body started to shake and vibrate. I felt a
very strong presence around me and through me, and I

received a download in the form of thoughts that came into my mind. I felt this presence to be Jesus because this is what the Voice said:

Tell the people that the reason I am not coming back is because I never left. I live within you. Treat everyone on any given day as though they were me; not because I am special, but because you are all so magnificent. Any time you feel any pain or suffering in any form, remember that it's the thoughts that cause you pain. Ask yourself, is this thought bringing me pain or joy? If it is pain, then decide for a new thought, and then thought by thought, remember the Truth.

That was it. My body was still vibrating, and continued to vibrate for about two hours after that. The message was so simple and loving, and kind. Then I remembered that the Course itself says "How simple is salvation! All it says is what was never true is not true now, and never will be. The impossible has not occurred and can have no effects."[2]

The difficulty lies in the fact that we do believe we are bodies and we have invested our belief in the world of bodies for a very long time from a linear perspective. So, to be told that we are not bodies and that nothing happened, meaning the separation from God hasn't really occurred, takes a bit more time to fully accept into our minds. That is understandable. But the ego, which is the thought of separation, is not understandable and never will be. It is literally unbelievable. Yet we still continue to believe in it. Why? There must be something we think it brings us, some benefit, something more than everything, and we want to be more than everywhere.

The ego, the false self-concept that we believe we are, split off from love and made a world that is separate from God, which is indeed everything and everywhere. The insane thought that fueled the ego is that it wanted to be the creator of itself and, therefore, attempted to usurp God's throne, which is a very silly idea, but one we bought into. As a result, the ego part of the split mind projected this world and bodies; bodies that appear to be both healthy and sick. That is duality, which is the nature of this world. In the *Course*, Jesus says there is no difference between a healthy body or a sick body because they are both untrue. It's still not reality, which is whole, perfect Oneness. So, a popular question among students who study the *Course* is what causes sickness and disease? In order to answer this question, I will discuss how health is defined in the Course, and then by natural extension, it will be revealed what the opposite of health represents.

Ralph Waldo Emerson once said, "The first wealth is health." I couldn't agree more. But most of us, when we think of health, think in terms of the body. If the body functions well, and is free of disease that means you are healthy. This is true in the way the world thinks of health, but this is just a small piece of what health represents.

The *Course* describes health as inner peace. If you are using the body for the Holy Spirit's purpose, which is to unite and become One, you are demonstrating your wholeness. Since you are a mind and not a body, you are uniting with the mind's purpose, which always represents oneness. The *Course* says, "The body, then, is not the source of its own health. The body's condition lies solely in your interpretation of its function."[3] Once your mind is healed it radiates health, and thereby teaches healing."[4]

These statements from the *Course* reflect Jesus's teaching that the mind is always the cause, and the body and the world are the effect. Our inner and outer worlds are the same, because the outside world is a pictorial representation of our thoughts projected outward. We are interpreting the body either with the ego or the Holy Spirit as our teacher. If health is inner peace, then you may be asking, how do I find it? The *Course* encourages us to practice true forgiveness, which is necessary to achieve the peace of God. True peace, which comes from true forgiveness, cannot come when anger is present. Anger is the opposite of peace, and anger is the ego's denial that peace exists, or else we would just choose it. Most people get angry at times, but the key is recognizing that anger is never justified, because we are never upset or angry for the reason we think. We are falsely perceiving people and the world, and simply cannot see the big picture, and therefore have no way of judging anyone or anything that would even come close to painting an accurate picture of what is going on.

As an aside to this, whenever we are trusting in our own strength, meaning with our ego as our teacher, it is inevitable that we would feel uncertain, anxious, and fearful. Putting our faith in the ego's false sense of strength is putting our faith in weakness. The *Course* is helping us to understand that God is our ultimate safety in every circumstance. This safety lies within us in our minds, and all we need to do is go past all our weak thoughts with the ego to the source of true strength. This place can be reached and can be counted on in every situation in which you find yourself. There is truly nothing to fear.

Forgiveness

Back to our question about how to find inner peace: Since true forgiveness is the necessary means to experience inner peace, which is being in a state of health, I will go over the steps of forgiveness as discussed in the *Course,* along with more specific commentary to explain the steps in greater detail. Before I do that, it would be helpful to clarify the difference between what the *Course* calls forgiveness-to-destroy and true forgiveness.

Forgiveness to Destroy

Forgiveness to destroy is the way most of the world thinks about forgiveness, which is that we forgive others for what they have really done, and in our minds we still think of them as guilty. This kind of forgiveness still makes the world real in the mind, which means that guilt is real. All we are doing when we attempt to forgive this way is reinforcing our own guilt since there is only one mind. All minds are joined. This is the key concept to understand in all your practicing with the *Course*. If there is only one mind, then any thought that you are putting out there to anyone else is going to you. To understand true forgiveness requires the basic understanding of how non-dualism works. There is only love, and nothing else. If we are being unloving by having fear thoughts about ourselves or others, we are in a state that does not exist. This takes time to accept through lots of patience and practice.

Forgiveness to destroy can mask itself in several different forms, and you will learn to recognize it by whether or not you are still holding any kind of grievance about the person or situation. If there is a part of you that still wants to think of someone as having done you wrong, maintaining the mindset that you are right, that is still forgiveness to destroy.

True Forgiveness

True forgiveness undoes the error we see in others and the world by letting go of our illusory interpretations and belief in separation. With true forgiveness, we are forgiving people not for what they've really done, but what they have *not* really done. The reason they have not done anything is because separation is an illusion, and we are still at home in God. Nothing happened, and our experience here in the world is only a dream. Events in a dream are not true, they are made up. To make someone guilty then is making the dream real and reinforcing the guilt in the mind that believes in separation. We can laugh away all our seriousness in the ego thought system, and replace it with Truth. Laughter is always helpful when it's not at someone else's expense, but rather a release from fear and intensity. Our special relationships with others are the most powerful opportunities we have to practice forgiveness. If you happen to be married, you may find this quote from Rodney Dangerfield amusing: "My wife and I were happy for twenty years. Then we met."

Please take note that true forgiveness is always done at the level of the mind and is not about behavior. So, this doesn't mean that you have to let someone walk all over you or abuse you in some way, brushing it aside and telling yourself you'll just keep allowing it to happen because you can just practice forgiveness. That wouldn't be very loving to yourself or to the person doing the abuse. So, you can still be normal and do the normal thing such as report abuse if you see it, but you can still practice forgiveness in your mind and have a deeper understanding about it, freeing yourself from the illusion of fear. There are definitely consequences in the world, and we are not asked to be passive to or condone abusive behavior, murders, crime, or any other treachery. We can practice forgiveness and let the love that comes from that inspire us to do what is most loving on this level in the world.

With this general background on both forgive-ness-to-destroy and true forgiveness, I will now go over the basic steps on how to truly forgive anyone or anything.

THE STEPS OF TRUE FORGIVENESS

Step 1: Identify the cause

The cause of any upset, no matter what form the upset takes, is our mind's choice for the ego's interpretation for what it is seeing, which is based on the *illusion* of separation. So, we are really upset because we are see-ing something that is not there; it's not true, and we are using what we dislike about a particular person or situation as an excuse to be separate from God, making our illusions real. **The key in this step is remembering that "I am doing this unto myself," realizing that what I am choosing is not making me happy. Once that is recognized, you will likely be more willing and open to another way of interpreting the situa-tion**. This first step may be expressed as innocently say-ing to yourself with a gentle smile: "There I go again, choosing the silliness of the ego." In other words, try to be playful about it. It's the seriousness in our minds that makes the world and our problems real. If you don't believe in God, you can think of God being per-fect love, which is what God is, which may make the ideas in this book more meaningful. The real problem is our fear of God, because we (the ego part of our split

mind) thought we attacked him by throwing his love
away, and then we made up a God in our own image;
one that is vengeful and is now going to punish us for
our "sin." The Course says that sin does not exist. Sin is
just a self-made concept, and has no relevance to reality
at all. Sin in the Course just means lack of love, or separation. We unconsciously believe we are sinful beings,
and that we are guilty, so it is this guilt that needs to
be undone.

Another way of looking at this first step is to
remember that you are dreaming.[5] You are dreaming a
dream of separation, which means you made up all of
the characters in your dream and are making them act
out for you, just as you do in your night time dreams.
You make them act out for you by your interpretation
of their purpose. If you see them as hateful and vicious
and guilty, that is how they will appear to you. In addition, since all minds are joined, that is how you will
see yourself. In this first step, you could simply just
remember you are dreaming a dream and the cause of
your upset is not outside of you, but in your mind.
Therefore you can change your mind about it and
choose a different teacher, the Holy Spirit, which will
remind you that you can see this person or situation
through the lens of love and innocence.

Jesus says that there are only two forms of expression: People are either expressing love or calling out
for it. If people are calling out for love, which can take
the form of vicious attacks, either physically or verbally,

then the proper response in your mind would be love, although physically it's wise to get out of harm's way and take care of yourself. When you choose to respond in your mind with loving thoughts, then you will naturally be guided as to what to do on the level of form (the world). This doesn't mean you have to be passive and let people walk all over you. It just means that you have chosen love in your mind first, and you will be able to respond, if needed, in a way that is loving instead of fearful. By practicing this kind of forgiveness you are undoing the guilt in your mind and reinforcing the peace and strength of God within you.

Step 2: Then let it (the cause) go so it can be replaced

As part of having a forgiving attitude, what this step entails is forgiving both your projected images and yourself for dreaming them.[6] So, you are forgiving your illusory perceptions, not the truth. The ego will want you to believe that what you are forgiving really happened, so you will believe you are forgiving what someone really said or did to you. To repeat, the *Course* says that we forgive people for what they *haven't* done, not what they *have* done. The reason they haven't done anything and they are innocent is because we didn't really separate from God's love. Try to remember the non-dualistic nature of God, that you can't really separate from His Love. This is a dream, and dreams aren't real. That is why we are all really innocent in reality. **So, the practice**

**of this step could take the form of saying to yourself:
"Holy Spirit, please help me to perceive this person
or situation through your Vision instead of my own.
I can choose peace instead of this."** This step takes
willingness to turn it over, and remind ourselves that we
don't know what's best, but the Holy Spirit does.

On the level of the world, there are consequences
of behavior, and that is the way the world is set up. But,
in your mind, you can know the truth. You and everyone else are really innocent and loved equally by God
because God created us all as One, and He created us to
be exactly the same as He is. We are his One Son. The
more you train your mind to think this way, the more
automatic your forgiveness will become. When we are
forgiving people for what they have really done, we
are making the error real, which makes the separation
more real in our minds. This forgiveness to destroy idea
takes many forms where it can trick you into thinking
you are really forgiving someone or something. You
will know if you have truly forgiven something if you
are completely free from fear of any kind, and peace is
in your awareness.

In this second step of forgiveness, what the ego
based thoughts are replaced with is the Holy Spirit's
thought system of wholeness, oneness and innocence,
which is already in your mind, and will happen naturally as an extension of the love of the Holy Spirit in
your mind. An example of how your thinking can be

reversed in this step is as follows: The statement "You are guilty and deserve to suffer" can be replaced with "You are spirit, whole and innocent. All is forgiven and released."[7]

So, this step is really about trusting in the Holy Spirit, and choosing His strength within you. Trusting in the Holy Spirit is trusting that He is in charge of the actual correction in the mind. Forgiveness *is* correction. You are responsible for just the first two steps, and then let the Holy Spirit handle the rest. The Holy Spirit will take your forgiveness and hold it in the one mind until it is ready to be accepted without fear. That is His job. Try to practice letting go of needing a certain result to take place. Remember, we don't really know what is best even for ourselves, let alone for anyone else, but we can ask the Holy Spirit to let whatever happens be for the highest good of all concerned.

With forgiveness, it is helpful to think in terms of wholeness and oneness. When *one* heals, we *all* heal. It is important to practice this kind of forgiveness on a daily basis, applying it to whatever comes up on any given day that disturbs your peace. Try not to exclude something because it seems minor to you. The seeming "little" things that disturb you affect your peace of mind just as much as those "bigger" things that seem harder. Practice seeing everything as the same. In other words, you are either at peace or you are not. There is no in-between. The *Course* says that there is no hierarchy of illusions. This means that there is not one problem bigger than another. The *Course* puts it this way, "There are no small upsets. They are all equally disturbing to my peace of mind."[8] But you don't have to leave it at that. Search your mind for all the attack thoughts that are causing you to suffer, and then remind yourself that you can change your mind. I'd also like to add that there is no hierarchy of ego or attack thoughts. They are all the same. They are either loving or they are not. This idea can help those who struggle with anxiety. I have some experience with anxiety which I will get into slightly in another chapter. If all attack thoughts are equal, then there cannot be one thought that is more intense or fearful than another. They can be looked at as all the same and all equally untrue. This takes practice because the mind has associated certain attack thoughts as being more fearful or real than others. You can gently remind yourself that this is a false idea, and practice reaching downward and inward to the strength of God in your mind where you are always safe.

Many people tell us in our workshops that they have a problem with self-forgiveness. They can forgive others, but have great difficulty forgiving themselves. The key to practicing self-forgiveness is remembering that ALL forgiveness is really self-forgiveness because there is only one mind. The ego believes that it is in a separated state, so it thinks of itself as disconnected to others. The belief in this separateness is the cause of lack of self-forgiveness. An idea that can be helpful to remember as you practice self-forgiveness (and will also be expanded on in the Light exercise in Chapter

6) is a question of purpose. Remind yourself that your purpose is not found in the body/personality as your identity. It is not found in illusions. Your purpose is beyond illusions, in your uniting with God. Most people still think they are forgiving their bodies. **With self-forgiveness, try practicing forgiving the *belief* that you are a body, and forgive your own illusory thoughts of attachment to the body as what you are. You might say, "I forgive myself for the belief that I am a body, that which can be separate from love. What I really am is perfect spirit, whole and inno-cent." Or, "I forgive myself for identifying with my attack thoughts that are taking the form of anxiety, depression, and holding grievances. Holy Spirit, help me to perceive myself as I really am, one with God, whole and innocent."** And leave it at that. The ego will want you to believe you have to do more. No more than this acknowledgement is required. Watch the temptation of the ego to try and make things more complicated. All forgiveness represents is a change of mind; a change of focus.

The benefits of practicing forgiveness are great. The results can show up in many different forms, but the one that I have noticed the most is that things show up in my life as symbols of my decision to think with the Holy Spirit, and having a forgiving attitude. For example, back in 2015 I started to develop severe allergies, which I later found out was an influence of global warming, and all of the different allergens, chemicals, and various substances in the environment. It affected my speaking voice, and I couldn't speak or sing for several months. I had to write all my thoughts down on little notepads. It was a strange feeling to not be able to use my voice, although Gary would joke, "We get along really great when you don't have a voice." I had a little bit of my voice, but it was very raspy and it was difficult to talk. In addition, it seemed as if I had a strange virus that affected my sinuses, so I was constantly stuffed up and blowing my nose day after day. It seemed as if this went on forever!

This was one of the more difficult times in my life, because I was right in the middle of recording my new CD, and I had to put it on hold. It was definitely a forgiveness opportunity, and I did practice looking at it differently. What choice did I have? To me, the choice was obvious. I had to surrender to it, and use what I have been taught in the Course; that I could practice being at peace regardless of circumstances. I believe it was my consistent practice and doing my best to not let it affect my peace, that it moved through my system quicker than it would have if I wasn't doing any forgiveness. Then, it showed up again in 2016, but this time it was much less severe, and I was able to use my voice, but my sinuses took a few months to clear. It's now 2017 as I write this, and…so far so good! Any positive results in my life are always attributed to forgiveness. I have come to understand that it's only in removing guilt from the mind that allows me to experience peace regardless of circumstances.

All this allergy stuff was new to me, since I hadn't experienced any major allergies since I was really young when I had to get allergy shots, remember those? But when something like this is used for forgiveness it becomes an opportunity to practice undoing the ego based thoughts, which in the long term has positive benefits at the mind level, which sometimes can result in relief on the physical level as well.

As a result of sticking with forgiveness during this whole process, things started showing up later on the level of form that were very helpful in assisting me in feeling well. A book on herbs and supplements would appear at the right time, or something I would hear on TV or from friends would be in sync with my thoughts on healing. Symbols were popping up in my dreams as well, with helpful information. This is what happens when more guilt is removed from the mind. Since you are more in touch with the love in your mind, you are naturally guided toward those things that will be helpful and loving. It's the thoughts that come first. When you change your mind to reflect the Holy Spirit's love and peace, the effect takes care of itself. This is why Jesus said, "You have sought first the Kingdom of Heaven, and all else has indeed been given you."[9] This is how you receive true inspiration, by joining with God and getting lost in His love. Then, let go and practice not being attached to results. It's the joining that matters. I will be discussing the exercise that goes along with this (called "True Prayer") in another chapter.

A more in-depth discussion on true forgiveness will be discussed in another book of this series, but for now, if you can apply these steps above to whatever is upsetting you, you will be making a lot of progress.

Sometimes the body may not appear to get better. It's helpful to remember that this doesn't mean it should be judged as bad. It's more helpful to practice letting go of your own judgment, and ask the Holy Spirit to judge rightly through you. His judgment would always see you as you are in Truth, whole and innocent in your oneness with God.

If any situation is used as an opportunity for forgiveness, it is furthering you along on the spiritual path. And, who can judge why someone's body may appear to get well, and another's doesn't? No one could possibly be in the position to judge accurately why a person's life script plays out the way it does. This is what we are doing - playing out our life scripts that were written at the instant we appeared to separate from God. When it comes to things that keep us rooted in the dream, the body is the star of the show. We place great value in the body, perceiving it as the cause of everything. Perhaps we are learning the difference between what is valuable and what is really valueless as it states in the *Course* under the "Development of Trust." Jesus says in his brilliant *Course*, "How can lack of value be perceived unless the perceiver is in a position where he must see things in a different light?"[10] So, whenever you are challenged by a health issue, be kind to yourself and patient. It may be one of the biggest learning opportunities you have to learn of what is truly valuable.

The body in and of itself isn't holy. When it is used for the Holy Spirit's purpose to let the Holy Spirit work through you and extend its love, it then serves a holy purpose. When the body serves the ego, it becomes sick. Sickness is not only an effect of separation...it *is* separation. In that sense, we are all sick on the mental level when we are perceiving wrongly because, again, only perception can be sick. Of course this sickness is projected out so the ego can see sickness everywhere but where it really is, in the mind. The ego made sickness as a defense against the Truth. It's as though we say defensively to the Creator, "It's okay; I'm sick; I've got it covered. Your punishment isn't necessary." This is insane. Separation itself is an insane idea, and no one who is really sane would need to incarnate. That being said, we can now take charge of our mind, recognizing that we can choose again what our reality is, with God. If we walk through our dreams with the Holy Spirit, with God as our Goal, we are walking with strength. Only the ego is weak, but you don't have to believe in it. The ego is not you. Invest your faith in the eternal, that which can't shift or change. You are then working your way to true health.

If these ideas seem scary to you now, the more you apply them and practice them in your everyday life, the more they become a part of your attitude of forgiveness, which undoes fear. You begin to identify yourself as Spirit, which is eternal, which is much more empowering than being a body that appears to be born, lives a while, then dies. There is no death. There is only life. Death, just like sickness, is a made up concept and is completely false. What you are, and always will be, is perfect Spirit, whole and innocent. Invest your faith in this, and you will be free!

CHAPTER 3

THE PURPOSE
OF THE BODY

*The body cannot heal, because it cannot make
itself sick. It needs no healing. Its health or sickness
depends entirely on how the mind perceives it, and
the purpose the mind would use it for.*[1]

One night in December of 2016, I awoke with a terrible headache. It was like a migraine type, a very painful pounding in my head. I figured I'd take a couple Tylenol to help, but I knew that it would take some time to work since this was a very intense headache. Before taking the Tylenol, I remembered to turn to the Holy Spirit first and ask for help. I thought of Archangel Raphael since he is the Angel of Healing, and for me, Angels are also a symbol of the love of the Holy Spirit.

Then, I let go and trusted, remembering that I can use the body for the Holy Spirit's purpose, which is to be a communication device to allow the love of the Holy Spirit to extend through me. I didn't know what form this channel would take at the time. I decided that I would take a Tylenol as well and then attempted to go back to sleep. As I was lying there in my bed, at the height of the head pain, Luna, my beautiful cat, who has shown healing abilities before, came right in and lay down right next to my neck and started purring really loud. I felt guided to place my hand on her back as she was purring and let the vibration of her purr move throughout my body, but more importantly, I imagined myself One with her and with the sound of the purr, the vibration, and with the Holy Spirit. About two minutes had passed, and I had just taken the Tylenol, not enough time for it to kick in. Luna got up after those two minutes, and sat at the end of the bed, and I noticed that my headache was completely gone. Not one trace of the pain remained. This happened in a matter of minutes once I first asked for help, then let go and waited for guidance. It was clear to me that Raphael, the angel of healing (which is also a symbol of the Holy Spirit) used Luna as a channel and extended Its Love through her to me in this amazing joining.

I don't know why this healing took place so fast this time since I had tried similar things before, but I imagine it was because I truly surrendered in that moment and just let go and trusted more, reminding myself of my true nature as Spirit. I also think the Holy Spirit wanted to reinforce in my mind the power of asking for help, which means you are not doing anything on your own. I had resigned as my own teacher in that moment and completely turned it over, knowing I would be okay regardless of what happened. Resigning as your own teacher and turning things over to the Holy Spirit is one of the ways of undoing the ego. This is because it was thinking that the ego knew best that got us all into this messy world in the first place, by acting on our own. Notice that there was no judgment about a part of my mind still using "magic" - a pill. But I was shown that relying on magic is unnecessary. And on the positive side, when we turn things over to the Holy Spirit, we are undoing the sense of separation, reminding the mind that we are not alone.

I share the story above to remind everyone of the power of remembering to ask for help. The Holy Spirit can and will use whatever channel is most helpful at the time to work its way into your experience. It can be through thought, a song, an image, a cat, or any other symbol. So, ask for help and trust. Let go without attachment to the form of how the healing might take place. It is very helpful to have the willingness to let go of our own ideas of how something should play out.

The real lesson is that even if the headache hadn't gone away, the work would still be to trust that it is being taken care of, and that you are under no laws but God's. The *Course* says, "There is nothing my Holiness cannot do."[2] This means that you are not at the effect of the laws of the world, and would do well not to look for salvation there. Jesus is teaching us that our salvation lies within, and that when we choose the teacher of love in our minds, we are joining with what we really are, and remembering God.

It is necessary to look at the dark thoughts in the mind, to notice them without judgment, and bring them to the light of truth. "No one can escape from illusions unless he looks at them, for not looking is the way they are protected."[3] This means that since we have made our illusions real, we must look at them first before we can see beyond them to Truth. This doesn't mean analyzing, but only looking without judgment. Healing is removing the blocks to the awareness of love's presence. Part of the work is replacing these ego based thoughts that are blocking love from entering with right-minded thoughts. Right-minded thoughts are those thoughts you are thinking with the Holy Spirit, having to do with love, peace, and innocence.

The *Course* also says that "The body's suffering is a mask the mind holds up to hide what really suffers."[4] In other words, the ego is using the body and its suffering as a defense mechanism to hide what we are *really* suffering from, which is the guilt over having chosen separation over wholeness, specialness over shared purpose, darkness over light, illusions over Truth. We, essentially, pushed God's love away and said that it wasn't enough, but then felt terrible guilt over that, and guilt demands punishment. So, we now projected our fear about this onto God and His Love, making God a punisher for our "sin," which didn't really happen. The world was then a projection of this guilt, and also a hiding place from God so we could never see his face. This is why we see "sin" in others, and make their errors real, because this is how the ego set it up so it wouldn't have to take responsibility for its thoughts of separation and the terrible guilt it felt. Projecting ourselves into a world of time and space is a clever way of forgetting this terrible feeling of "sin," which was really just a mistake. **Let us remember that there is no sin; only a belief in sin.**

Since we believe the separation from God happened, we have now become confused about the purpose of the body, and have been using it for the ego's purpose since the beginning of time. We have simply forgot what we are and where we came from. We may have forgotten our Source, which is love, but love has not forgotten *us*. Forgetting our Source produces fear in the unconscious mind. If we are afraid, we are placing more value on the things that keep us in the dark. We can change our minds and choose peace instead. True peace that passeth understanding can't be penetrated by guilt. "It denies the ability of anything not of God to affect you. This is the proper use of denial."[5] Just as this is the proper use of denial, there is also a proper use for separation: Separating out the false from the true.

Most of us believe we are bodies, so we are not being asked to deny that experience, but to shift the purpose of what it is for. It's not about denying your worldly experience. In other words, it's okay to live your normal life and do the things you'd normally do, but now you can do it with the Holy Spirit as your guide and experience peace instead of fear.

I have heard many people say they have stopped taking their medications or refuse to take medications because the body is just an illusion, even though those medications were helpful. Some even appeared to suffer more when off the medications, but they still insisted on not taking them. Attempting to prove that you don't need medications because the body isn't real just makes the ego thought system more real in your mind, and reinforces guilt. The point is that whatever you decide, try to practice doing it without guilt. Denying the body experience when you still believe you are a body can create tremendous conflict if you are trying to prove that you don't need something by telling yourself forgiveness will take it all away. What forgiveness will do is return your mind to a condition of peace, and sometimes the body issue does go away, and sometimes it doesn't, but when your mind is at peace, it won't matter either way. That is the goal.

Sometimes certain medications may not be the best choice, and you will know by how you feel. It's important to notice what is working and what is not. I have experienced tremendous anxiety in my life starting at age 15. When I was in my 20's it escalated to where I was having consistent panic attacks. It got so intense that I finally decided to try medication, even though

I usually resisted taking medication. At the time, my doctor put me on Ativan for panic attacks. It was a terrible experience for me! Although it helped a bit with the anxiety, the side effects were awful, and I noticed I was becoming very depressed. This was a case where medication seemed to be working against me. This wasn't just a low-lying depression. I didn't want to get out of bed in the mornings and I had no motivation to do anything. I would cry on a whim for no apparent reason, and I was very fearful of going outside. It felt like I was having a nervous breakdown. This lasted for two weeks, which is all I could take. I decided to go off the Ativan, and I started to balance out again, just taking things day by day. I wasn't practicing forgiveness at the time because I wasn't doing the *Course* yet. But I got through it with faith and determination not to let it bring me down. Those that know me know that I've always been a positive person by nature. I've been that way my whole life. I think that has served me well in the most difficult times. Just being positive on its own isn't the answer to suffering, but it does help. Also, it is very important to have support when you are going through something traumatic. Being around others who are loving and understanding, and offering general support, can truly help move you through difficult situations. I did have support, and that helped a lot.

Later, when I looked back on that experience, I realized that all of us have this tremendous strength to get through seemingly very dark times. What is it that gets us through? Somewhere in our minds we know the Truth. We remember that we are as God Created us, perfect, whole, and innocent. It is an underlying feeling that we are taken care of no matter what. This memory exists in all of us, and it is this strength that gets us through the most difficult of times even if we don't understand where it comes from. For me, I had tremendous faith that things would be okay even though I didn't know exactly what steps to take. The anxiety became more free-floating from that point on, with a couple intense experiences later on. Now I have learned to manage it through forgiveness and changing my mind about it.

Many people experience different forms of depression and anxiety. The real cause, however, remains blocked because most people are unaware of what causes depression and its various cousins. Lesson 41 in the workbook of the *Course* says "Depression is an inevitable consequence of separation. So are anxiety, worry, a deep sense of helplessness, misery, suffering and intense fear of loss."[6] The *Course* teaches that there is a way out of this misery. We all have the Light within, that which we all are in Truth. Accessing the truth within is what heals the mind that believes in these many miserable forms of separation. In another chapter, I will discuss some of the exercises that undo this sense of guilt and separation that is the cause of so much suffering.

In keeping with the non-dualistic nature of the *Course's* thought system, it would also have to follow that what we think is the problem of our suffering is not even a "real" problem. This is because separation itself is impossible. This is also why the *Course* says "A sense of separation from God is the only lack you really need correct."[7] It is this deep feeling of separation that caused us to feel lack for the first time, which then got projected out into thousands of different forms and fragments, making it seem like there were levels of need and orders of difficulty, where one thing is bigger or harder to overcome than another. This may bring up intense anxiety at first because we are all so trained and conditioned to believe the opposite. We truly believe that unless we obey certain laws of the world, we will die, when the *Course* is saying that you are not a body and death is not real. It's wise to follow the basic laws of the world, though, as long as we believe we are bodies or else we will experience not so nice consequences on the level of form. It's not until you become a true master like Jesus that you can experience total and complete peace all the time, and not feel any pain. We can achieve this, but it takes great willingness to want peace above all else. It is already our experience in reality, but we are awakening to that. That experience in my 20's taught me that the strength of God in me is far more powerful than the puny little ego. If we have the willingness to allow God into our minds, we are well on our way to healing.

During that time of anxiety, I had a profound dream. I was lying in my bed, drifting off to sleep. I started to feel a sensation of "slipping away." I felt as though I was sinking into my bed. It actually felt like

I was dying, like a letting go. Then, everything in my vision became very dark. But it wasn't a fearful dark, just total blackness, but peaceful. A spark of light appeared in my vision in the middle of the blackness. A male voice spoke to me and said, "Let God into your heart." It was very profound. I'll never forget it. I opened my eyes and felt a tremendous peace, like I was being taken care of and totally loved. It made me very aware that I had not been good to myself, had not been very loving toward myself. I consider that experience to be one of the catalysts for my turning more inward and encouraging my search for Truth. It wasn't too long after that when I found the *Course*. I knew that it was going to be my path, and everything about it resonated with me. I know a lot of people experience the same feelings when they first discover the *Course*. It's like "Finally! This explains it all, and makes perfect sense! God could not have created a world of pain and suffering!"

In regards to the above story about anxiety, there is a section in the *Course* called "Littleness vs. Magnitude."[8] Many of us play small and hide our light for fear of shining too brightly. I was an expert at this, dimming my light to make others feel better. The *Course* says that we are not worthy of playing small. We are worth much more than that! We are worth the consistent effort. The magnitude of what we really are is beyond comprehension. As we continue undoing layers of guilt, this light becomes more dominant and we are becoming more of what we really are in Truth. The Light is always there, but it gets blocked by the dark clouds of guilt. This is why the *Course* emphasizes forgiveness. **It is true forgiveness that undoes the guilt.**

Holy Spirit's Purpose for the Body

Now let's come back to purpose, to shed some light on how we can use our experiences here for the highest good of all concerned. The *Course* instructs us that there are two purposes for the body, but only one of them is truly helpful. The Holy Spirit's purpose for the body, which is always helpful if we use it in this way, is to use it as a communication device. What is communicated is the Holy Spirit's love, peace, and innocence extending through us, so we can become channels of His Love, extending this love to our brothers and sisters. This is how we truly join with our brothers and sisters. Most people do not use the body for this purpose because they have become confused about its true function. The body's only real value is using it to join in the mind with others and with the Holy Spirit. Otherwise, it has no value. I know this may seem harsh and even bring up uncomfortable feelings because we are so conditioned to make the body important and valuable. To say otherwise is blasphemous to the ego! Everything in the world centers around the body, and in making it look and feel good. The body is the hero of the dream, as the *Course* puts it.

If you start using the body for the Holy Spirit's purposes, you will stop using it to attack yourself and others. These attacks take the form of Judgment and condemnation, which is a projection of the guilt in the unconscious mind. The Holy Spirit *only* sees you as you really are in Truth, and that is why you can trust Him as you look to Him to teach you what you are through joining with others. As we look upon other bodies, we see only our interpretation of them; nothing else. We give everyone and everything all the meaning that it has for us, and as we see other people, that is how we see ourselves. This is why it is very wise to watch your thoughts and particularly pay attention to the thoughts you are thinking daily about other people. Since minds are joined, any message you are sending out makes a statement about what you really believe about yourself. The *Course* calls it our "secret sins and hidden hates"[9] that we project onto others, but secretly believe to be about ourselves. These "attack" thoughts we project onto others, but are really in our own minds, is also part of what causes depression. It comes from separation. When we are thinking "attack" thoughts we are separating from God's love and therefore experiencing ourselves as lacking. To correct this lack we must replace the ego thought system with the thought system of the Holy Spirit. We have to catch ourselves and look at what we are doing to ourselves. We must begin to hear the same old tape we are playing in our minds that keeps us in mental pain. The effects of a deprived mind show up in thousands of different forms, stemming from guilt that includes illness and all forms of disease, unhappiness, sadness, fear, worry, anxiety and depression.

What a blessing to know that regardless of what goes on with our bodies or the world, we are still innocent! That is why no one should feel bad or guilty if they get sick. Bodies show the symptoms of sickness sometimes because that is how the ego set it up. Now we have another way of looking at the body. We can remember that it's not who we really are, and that if the body is in our mind, we can change our mind about it.

The Ego's Purpose for the Body

The ego, wanting the separation from God to be true so it can be special, uses the body for another purpose. The body is a symbol of separation, so therefore the ego uses the body to make itself sick in thousands of different forms as a defense against the truth of our oneness. To the ego, the body is to attack *with* − it equates us with the body. Probably without realizing it, Jackie Mason (an American Rabbi and comedian) summed up the ego's purpose brilliantly: "It's no longer a question of staying healthy. It's a question of finding a sickness you like." This body is not our reality. To repeat an important point, this doesn't mean you should feel guilty if you get sick. The script is written. "For we but see the journey from the point at which it ended, looking back on it, imagining we make it once again; reviewing mentally what has gone by."[10] This concept can explain the deja-vu experience. We, literally, are mentally reviewing the scripts of our lives, like playing an old tape. It has already happened. Of course we would have glimpses or feelings that something has happened before, because we have watched it before in our minds. But now we appear to be experiencing it all over again. This can help us to remember it's all a dream, and that this dream is already over.

Returning to the ego's purpose, the reason we attack others and think it is justified is that we think it brings us something we want. But remember, we have become confused about what it is we really want, and what brings us true joy. The ego confuses pain and pleasure, and this is always the result of making a false association, but it is also the very foundation of the ego thought system: thinking that we know what's best for us, that we are always right. This is insane. We have no basis for judging what is right or holy, except by changing our minds to start learning with a different teacher, one who does know everything - the Holy Spirit.

Unconscious to us, the ego invests in sickness, because this is its way of stating that you are not invulnerable. At times, we all feel vulnerable to sickness, and no one here is perfect. But you can practice not letting this ego device of sickness trick you into thinking that you can really be attacked or hurt by something or someone outside of yourself. That is a decision. In other words, always remember that you can use any form of attack or sickness for a different purpose, as an opportunity to see things in a different light, to remember that what you really are cannot be hurt or attacked in any way. If you do not believe this yet, let's remember that the training of the mind is a process involving a huge shift, the whole point being to get in touch with your mind's power to choose how you are interpreting anything. This power to choose, which is the one remaining freedom we have, will be discussed in greater length in another chapter.

As I said earlier, there may be times when the body appears to get well as a result of practicing forgiveness, and there may be times when it doesn't. We are in no position to judge what is best because we can't see the whole picture. We are being taught in the *Course* that the choice to judge is the cause of the loss of peace. The best thing we could ever do no matter what goes on with our bodies is to let go of judgment and let the Holy Spirit be the judge for us. The Holy Spirit's judgment is always the same: You are an innocent Son of God, perfect in His sight. There is no sin, and you never left your home in Heaven. "You are at home in God, dreaming of exile but perfectly capable of awakening to reality."[11]

As *Course* students, the more we practice these ideas, the more we are reinforcing them in our minds and helping others to choose the same. Health is joining. Sickness is separation. The goal of the *Course* is to experience peace regardless of what is going on in the world or in your body. That is true power; the power to choose peace under any and all circumstances.

Removing the blocks to the awareness of our true nature is the way to health and well-being. To be free of all illusions is to withdraw your belief from them, and invest in what is wholly true. When we realize the non-dualistic nature of reality, that only wholeness and oneness is true, then it would have to follow that anything that appears to be the opposite must be an illusion.

"If you remain as God created you, appearances cannot replace the truth, health cannot turn to sickness, nor can death be substitute for life, or fear for love."[12] What is happening is that we are having a dream of sickness and a dream of health. Once we accept this is all a dream, we don't have to let the dream affect the peace of God in our minds. This is not always easy to practice because we have become so invested in the ego as our identity. However, if we have the willingness to let that go, and decide that there is another way of looking at things and at the body and the world, peace will come. It comes with patience, practice, and willingness.

CHAPTER 4

THE POWER
OF CHOICE

Choosing Between Separation
and Wholeness

*You always choose between your weakness and
the strength of Christ in you. And what you
choose is what you think is real.*[1]

One day in the early part of the year of 2015, in the height of my strange allergy/virus situation, I started to panic because I felt that it was hard for me to breathe. I went into the office where Gary was working and explained to him in a panicked way that I was struggling to breathe normally. This was also the time when

I had lost my voice, so I wasn't talking much during this time, which made it harder for me to express myself. I said to Gary in my very hoarse voice, "Please call the doctor, and tell him I am having trouble breathing!" During this moment, something told me that it wasn't as bad as I was making it out to be. It was all in my mind, and that everything would be okay. My thoughts were making the situation worse. Although I heard that whisper in my ear I was still panicking. I did the "normal" thing and still had Gary call the doctor, just in case. The doctor explained that my symptoms were part of a normal process of one dealing with allergies. That didn't comfort me much because I was making the whole situation real in my mind by continuing to think of negative outcomes, like what if I pass out? What if I have to go to the hospital? What if…what if…what if…!! These "what if's" were only contributing to the panic and making the world real. The doctor went ahead and prescribed something for me that would help with my breathing and clear my sinuses. He didn't seem the least bit concerned.

After I got off the phone with him, I realized something: The fact that both Gary and the doctor remained so calm during this episode, all the while being helpful, started to remind my mind that the separation was not real. I went into the other room, and started to calm down. I started to remember my power of choice. I could continue thinking of myself as a vulnerable body, identifying with the ego, or I could choose the strength of Christ in me, and be vigilant *only* for God and His

Kingdom. As soon as I started having right-minded thoughts, I started to feel better. I even remembered to laugh. I recognized that no matter what is happening, I can still choose what I would have myself be: A body or Spirit. I chose Spirit from that moment on.

This experience also reminded me of the power of being in the presence of others who are in their right minds when you are going through something that seems traumatic. Their demonstration of peace reminds the mind that what it is experiencing here is not true. There is no separation, and what you really are cannot be hurt in any way. This is very helpful at the mind level. Of course, as in my situation, both Gary and the doctor still did the "normal" thing and responded in a helpful way at the level of form as well. If there truly was an emergency, Gary would have called 911, and wouldn't hesitate. One can still go about doing those "normal" things in the dream while remaining in their right minds, which is doing it with the strength of God in you, rather than with the weakness of the ego. This experience really helped to reinforce these ideas even more, and I felt much more determined to not let anything disturb my peace.

In light of all that has been discussed so far, I would like to make it very clear that most of what has been said has been about the mind, and how you can start to look at your life, body, and the world from a different perspective. This is because the *Course* is a thought system, a mind-training document. Practicing its principles will inevitably result in seeing your apparent life here from a new perspective. You do not stop taking care of the body, going to your doctor, or doing what you would normally do. There is a line in the *Course* that says, "I need do nothing."[2] This statement is often mis-interpreted to mean that you just remain passive when it comes to the body, deny the body experience, and just wait around for something to happen to you. This approach would not be very helpful if you did, in fact, have an emergency. No, the *Course* explains further. "To do nothing is to rest, and make a place within you where the activity of the body ceases to demand atten-tion. Into this place the Holy Spirit comes, and there abides."[3] And, "This quiet center, in which you do noth-ing, will remain with you, giving you rest in the midst of every busy doing on which you are sent. For from this center will you be directed how to use the body sinlessly."[4] What you do want to do is undo the ego thought system, practice forgiveness, and continue to remain passive to the ego, but active to the Holy Spirit. This process helps you to withdraw your belief in the ego being your identity, and you will more likely act from a place of inspiration instead of fear.

Another way of looking at the line "I need do nothing" is to think of the idea again that you are a mind and not a body. The mind is outside of time and space, and the strength of God resides within the mind that you have access to at any time. So, all we need to do is accept that God's strength is already within us to choose. When you allow the Holy Spirit to guide you, then whatever you do comes from a place of inspiration and love instead of attack, condemnation, and judgment. In other words, this quiet center the Course speaks of is a place in your mind that you can always return to in the midst of the seeming turmoil around you, and when the chaotic happenings of life overwhelm you.

As a metaphor, think of a very large superstorm, like a hurricane, and the eye of the hurricane is the calm center, and it's only on the outside where the chaos appears to be, with all its dark clouds, howling winds, and roaring waters. *You* are really this calm center, and nothing on the outside can hurt you. The outside picture is a representation of your thoughts projected outward. But these thoughts aren't reality, and can have no effect on you unless you give them the power, by making them real. Think of this calm center, the eye, as the Light of Truth that abides within you, and it is here where your decision-maker lives. It is here that you have the power to choose with which teacher you will view the seeming outside swirling clouds. You are always choosing between the ego, which speaks for separation, or the Holy Spirit, which speaks for Wholeness and Oneness. Whichever teacher you choose will be the basis for how you interpret what appears to be outside of you.

Remember, what you are seeing on the outside is only an effect of your thoughts, not the cause of them. The outside world is a pictorial representation of your inner world. You always see what you want to see. This is true because the dream is coming *from* you, not *at* you. The one mind is dreaming a dream, and the more you think of yourself as this one mind, you will see how it all fits together. Important note: **This doesn't mean that you are personally responsible for other people's behavior.** You are only responsible for how you are looking at or interpreting everything. Behavior is an effect of thought. We first think a thought, then feel a feeling, then act it out. If you practice getting in touch with the thought behind it all first, you can then begin to take control of your power to choose. This is real power, not some kind of false power that says you are bigger or better than somebody else because of your worldly position or spiritual progress.

The *Course* tells us that there is a danger in thinking that we are advanced beyond what we can even understand, or that we can judge anyone or anything with any accuracy, or that we have any idea of how to transform our dreams of fear into happy dreams. We are encouraged to always put the Holy Spirit in charge of this. In fact, the *Course* says, "Some of your greatest advances you have judged as failures, and some of your deepest retreats you have evaluated as success."[4] I find this to be very humbling.

In the *Course*, Jesus speaks of being like little children. He says, "Little children recognize that they do not understand what they perceive, and so they ask what it means. Do not make the mistake of believing that you understand what you perceive, for its meaning is lost to you."[5] He is saying that we can't know or even understand what anything means because what we are seeing with the body's eyes is not true. We are misperceiving everything around us. It's just a projection coming from the ego part of the split mind. We can't even know what we want or what is best for us because we have conflicting wishes, which is an effect of a split mind. To be truly innocent is to be free of the ego's perception. This reminds me of the innocence of a child's thinking in the following joke: A Sunday school teacher asked her children as they were on the way to church service, "And why is it necessary to be quiet in church?" One bright little girl replied, "Because people are sleeping."

Back to the split mind, the good news is that by practicing the Holy Spirit's magnificent tool of true forgiveness, we are contributing to the healing of the split mind and making ourselves whole again.

I was doing a workbook lesson in the *Course*, and the exercise was to search my mind for my reactions to various situations, making no distinctions between positive and negative because they are both untrue. I had done this exercise before, but it hit me more deeply this time (a common experience of *Course* students). I really realized that my mind was full of conflicting thoughts and wishes. I would see myself having an attribute that appeared to be negative, then a minute later I would come up with something positive. This went back and forth for five minutes. It really hit home to me that no wonder the ego is so confused and confusing! The mind being split will always be a dualistic mind until each one of us truly wants to hear only one voice; the voice of the Holy Spirit. Jesus says: "When you want only love you will see nothing else."[6] And, "The power of decision is your one remaining freedom as a prisoner of this world. You can decide to see it right."[7] We have to have abundant willingness to stay on course and watch our thoughts and reactions to various events on a consistent basis. This takes work, but in my opinion it is worth everything to have the peace of God above all else. Many of us want the peace of God, but don't really do the work and practice it takes to get there. Just saying something is a forgiveness opportunity is not practicing forgiveness. We are being encouraged to actually do each step of forgiveness, applying it to everyday situations, people, and events that disturb our peace.

Something that can be helpful as you practice making the choice for which teacher you are choosing to interpret anything with is to remember the idea that there are always only two forms of expression, no matter what appears to going on. People are either expressing love, or calling out for love. There is no in between. This is why there are only two emotions: Love and fear, but only one of them is true. The ego made fear, and love was given to us by God because he created us to be exactly the same as He is. When you choose to see all forms of fear as a call for love, you are more likely to move into a place of compassion instead of anger. When you choose to see fear as an attack upon you, your experience will reflect that. When you see only love, your experience will be loving. At any time you feel the temptation to condemn or judge someone else for their behavior, to think unloving thoughts about them, simply ask yourself, "Would I condemn myself for doing this?"[8] If you hold another person prisoner in your mind, which means you are making that person the cause of your upset, and coming from separation, then you are also imprisoning yourself because you share the same mind. You cannot see that this is so, but it is true. You will know by how you feel. Your mood will tell you which teacher you have chosen every single time. This is why feelings can be helpful. If we remember that perception is interpretation (not fact), then it naturally follows that it is the way we are interpreting something that brings forth positive or negative emotions. If you get angry, you are responding to an interpretation you made, which you have then projected onto someone or something seemingly outside of you.

Feelings

Many people ask how feelings come into play, and are they important. They are important in the sense that you can use them as a meter to determine which teacher you have chosen in your mind. If you feel bad, that's the ego. If you feel peace, that's the Holy Spirit. It is important to express your feelings, but without projecting them onto other people or yourself. The way to do this is to notice the feelings when they come up without denying them, and just look at them with the Holy Spirit, which is looking without judgment. When we judge ourselves or others, we lose our peace, since the choice to judge is the cause of the loss of peace. If you let the Holy Spirit be the judge through you, He will judge truly, which means He will see only innocence everywhere. It is okay to express your feelings to others, but it is more helpful to practice doing it without attacking or blaming, making others the cause of your upset. There is a difference between just sharing what is going on with you and blaming someone else. You may even find you can create a "win-win" situation where all parties involved benefit.

There is a saying in the *Course* which I find very helpful in dealing with any form of upset. It says, "I do not know what anything including this means. And so I do not know how to respond to it. And I will not use my own past learning as the light to guide me now."[9] The ego part of the split mind thinks of everything in terms of the past, because it thinks it sinned in the past, then made that idea very real by projecting it outside itself. This is why everything here in the world is based upon the past. We've become attached to it. Every upset or judgment we have about ourselves or other people are based on the past ideas of sin, guilt, and fear which the ego made up at the instant of separation from God. This also explains why we don't really see the present, which represents total Truth. We are identified with the past and therefore do not see reality. The miracle in the *Course*, which is a shift in perception which happens when we practice true forgiveness, enables us to let go of seeing others from the past, so we can perceive them as they really are. **Let us be reminded that this world is already over, and that we are mentally reviewing that which has already gone by. We only need to accept the correction, which is already there in the mind because God placed it there by giving us His Holy Spirit; the answer to the separation**.

With practice, you will get better and better at being able to tell the difference between the ego and the Holy Spirit. It really comes down to how important having a peaceful mind is to you. Most people say they want to be at peace, but don't really know how to get there. The *Course* tells us how. Peace comes from true forgiveness as was discussed in a previous chapter. It takes great willingness to practice right-minded ideas on a daily basis, but doesn't everything take practice if you want to be good at it? Have no fear, for you will not be asked to go directly to the light before you are ready to do so. This is why the *Course* is leading us to a happy dream, which precedes our awakening from the dream. This is a necessary step in the process.

The mind must be returned to a condition of peace before it can enter the kingdom of Heaven or it would be too fearful. We wouldn't even feel comfortable or ready to enter the Kingdom of God as long as there is guilt in the mind. An analogy would be that if you were learning to play the piano, and today was your first lesson. Then, right after your first lesson the teacher says, "Okay, tonight you will be playing a concert of compositions by Mozart." I think anybody in that position would be pretty freaked out because they know they wouldn't be ready for that. This is what it would be like to be thrust into reality, the state of Heaven's perfect Oneness, before we are ready. I am speaking here of the ultimate awakening, not the in-between lives, which everyone appears to experience each time they pass away before going into another body. I am speaking of the readiness for God, for his perfect Oneness, all that is, and the only thing that's real. This is experienced when the guilt in the unconscious mind has been completely forgiven.

In the in-between life it is still not Heaven's perfect oneness, and you are still experiencing a dream of separation as long as you appear to see images and think of yourself as being an individual soul. You may perceive lots of different images, nature scenes, and geographical locations, as well as various colors and other beings that appear to be separate from you. These can be lovely experiences, but the *Course* says that "All your time is spent in dreaming. Your sleeping and your waking dreams have different forms and that is all. Their content is the same."[10] This includes when you appear to be awake, when you appear to be sleeping, and in the afterlife, in between incarnations. You are always being guided, but it is not until you have transcended the world entirely and the need to incarnate, that you are re-joined with God in perfect oneness, where that is your *only* reality. You can still experience revelation while you appear to be here, and have an experience of oneness with God, but it will be temporary until you have awakened from the dream.

All of us experience what we think of as challenges in life from time to time, and it may seem like certain things that disturb you just don't stop or go away. You may even be forgiving something over and over, and the same situation just keeps happening, making it seem like your forgiveness isn't working. Do not let this stop you from practicing and applying forgiveness to everything that comes up. Instead, remember this from the *Course,* "Trials are but lessons that you failed to learn presented once again, so where you made a faulty choice before you now can make a better one, and thus escape all pain that what you chose before has brought to you. In every difficulty, all distress, and each perplexity Christ calls to you and gently says, "My brother, choose again.""[11] This is how you release your mind from fear, when you remember that you are not powerless in the face of great challenges. You can decide to see it right, with your right mind. Your peace depends on it. And you must desire peace above all else. The *Course* says that when you say you want the peace of God, "To say these words is nothing. But to mean these words is everything."[12] When you truly mean you want the peace of God, you will demonstrate it by practicing forgiveness. You are demonstrating what kind of a teacher you are at any given moment by which teacher in your mind you are listening to. This is the choice you have, and you use your mind to choose between the body and Spirit. When you get in touch with your mind's power to choose, you realize that you never have to be a victim of the world you see.

Jesus isn't saying that you have to give up the world or give up your life you made here, but you will be much happier when you give up your attachment to the world you now see through the lens of the ego. The irony is that as you progress on your spiritual path, you will start seeing the world more and more like a dream that you *want* to awaken from. A non-dualistic path is not about being more awake *in* the dream, but awakening *from* the dream. **When Jesus says to renounce the world, and make it meaningless, he is saying to let go of the meaning that *you* gave it and let the Holy Spirit's word be written in its place**. So, to reiterate an important point, this doesn't mean that you have to give up all the nice things that you may experience here. It's more about the choosing to walk in the world, but with a different purpose, to be truly helpful; to let everything you do be used for the Holy Spirit's purpose and not your own.

I would like to share some examples of how I used my mind's power to choose between the ego and the Holy Spirit. When Gary and I first met back in 2006, we were 20 years apart in age. I guess that means we are still 20 years apart, that still hasn't changed! There were a few people now and then who thought I was much younger than I was, although I was 35 when I met Gary. Although to me that was a compliment, some people would give us interesting looks, like are those two really together? What, is she 22 or something? And because I dressed a bit more modern, not as conservative as some might expect in the spiritual community, there were some who actually approached me and said I should dress more like a spiritual teacher. I actually found that amusing because I was thinking, "Oh, how is a spiritual person supposed to dress? Is there a dress code or something? If so, I didn't get that memo." Later, a few people apologized for their judgments even though I didn't even know about them, but in my mind I wasn't offended at all by what they thought. I just saw it as an opportunity to see them as whole and innocent, remembering that all people are images being projected from the one mind, and it was totally my responsibility how I chose to think about them. This was a clear opportunity to practice the *Course's* thought system.

One day I received an email from someone I'd never met. This person wrote, "I know that you married Gary for his money." My first thought was, "What money?" This provided a moment of hilarity for me and my husband (and we were not laughing *at* anyone). We often joke about the perception that because you are a best-selling author, you are wealthy. This is not always the case. We do fine, but we are not rich. By the time you read these words, maybe our situation will have changed and we will be super rich. It doesn't matter. The point is that this person made a judgment which the world in general would consider an attack. I could have chosen to be offended. But I was practicing the *Course* enough by this time to remember that nothing happened. This comment was really a call for love in disguise. I saw him as innocent, whole and perfect. I emailed him back a short, polite email saying "Thank you for sharing your feelings with me. I want you to know that whatever you say or do won't change my mind about you. I will not be tricked into thinking you are anything less than what God created you to be. You are always a brother. Perhaps we will meet one day. Thank you again for sharing." He emailed me back an even shorter email this time and said, "I see you have the kindness thing down." I responded with wishing him well, and then I never heard from him again. In this situation, I chose to say these particular words to him, but I could have just said them in my mind and that would have been fine. I felt guided to let him know verbally that his opinion didn't change my mind about him or his reality as perfect Spirit, which was really reminding my own mind that I am perfect Spirit.

When this happened, please note that I said I could have *chosen* to be offended. Then my response would have been much different. Instead, I chose peace. That was and has been more important to me than anything else. By remembering what you are in truth, that you are as God Created you, then you could *never* be offended by anyone or anything. When we identify with our egos, then there is no choice but to be at the effect of the world. What you really are is in no need of defense.

You can only be attacked by your own choice. Yes, the body can be attacked and it is appropriate to protect yourself from physical harm. At the same time you can remember what I quoted earlier, "You are not a body. You are love, and it matters not where love appears to be, for being love, it cannot be wrong."[13]

This shift in thinking, making the choice for wholeness rather than separation, is part of how you develop a healthy state of mind. **Remember, health is inner peace**. When you are well in your mind, you will experience *well-being*. To repeat an important point, only the mind can be sick. This doesn't mean that you shouldn't be appropriate when you are in the presence of someone who is physically sick. Kindness is the guideline here. In other words, it might not be helpful to just start quoting the *Course* to them, or trying to convince them they shouldn't be sick because sickness is a defense against the truth. Would this have helped you when you were feeling bad or down about yourself?

Everyone gets sick in some form from time to time, because the script was written at the seeming beginning of time. We are now just mentally reviewing the script from another level. Our work is really choosing how we look at it *now*. Please don't feel guilty if you get sick. That will only feed the ego, which is what it wants. When you are with someone who is sick, you don't have to worry about what to say or do. When you choose the teacher of love first in your mind, then let go, you will be guided as to the most loving thing to say or do, if anything. You might just be present with the person, letting go of all judgment of their condition as good or bad, but see them with true perception, through the eyes of the Holy Spirit, which knows only their wholeness. This love may take the form of giving them a hug, or just hanging out and having a normal conversation. Love can take many forms, but when you let love be your guide, you can let go of any worry about what to do or how to act.

Making the choice for wholeness over separation directly relates to healing. In the "Song of Prayer," a supplement of the *Course*, Jesus says, "Sickness and separation must be healed by love and union."[14] This section explains that what we appear to do as humans is substitute one illusion for a seeming "nicer"one; "a dream of sickness for a dream of health."[15] But when we use illusions to heal illusions, we don't get very far, and the healing is usually not permanent. This is what the *Course* calls false healing. False healing can appear to be effective, and symptoms may go away for a time. The *Course* says "But the cause remains, and will not lack effects. The cause is still the wish to die and overcome the Christ."[16] This thought is unconscious to us, so it might sound preposterous at first. It takes some spiritual experience and practice before this idea is truly accepted. Many things sound preposterous when we don't have true understanding. We thought it was preposterous when it was insinuated that the world was round and not flat, or the idea that someone could walk on the moon. It's preposterous until we have some sort of experience that tells us a different story. But the statement above reflects the idea that the ego wants to be a special, individual self, something greater than reality with God, and this was the idea the ego had when it first chose the separation from God at the beginning before a world of time and space appeared to be here. This false sense of individuality and specialness is what we are now being asked to undo. The *Course* is all about undoing the ego to achieve true peace. True peace will come from true understanding. True understanding comes from undoing the ego by practicing forgiveness.

As the mind begins to awaken, you may find that you are more open-minded in general, and have less judgment. Open-mindedness is one of the characteristics of God's teachers as stated in the "Manual for Teachers" in the *Course*. Open-mindedness allows you to be open to inviting the Holy Spirit into your mind. Remember the superstorm/hurricane analogy? Well, open-mindedness diminishes the swirling, dark clouds so that Christ's face is seen again. You will also begin to notice, with practice, that things that used to upset you do not have the same impact on you anymore. This means the mind is becoming more peaceful. You are learning to see with true vision and think like the Holy Spirit thinks. It's helpful to think of everything that disturbs you as an opportunity to practice seeing with true vision, without any judgment. Vision has nothing to do with the body's eyes; rather, it is how you are thinking. This can literally change the quality of experience you are having in any given moment. "A tranquil mind is not a little gift."[17]

It is also helpful to start a process of inner questioning, diving a bit deeper into the nature of things. In another supplement to the *Course* called "Psychotherapy: Purpose, Process, and Practice," Jesus says that "Healing occurs as a patient begins to hear the dirge he sings, and questions its validity. Until he hears it, he cannot understand that it is he who sings it to himself. To hear it is the first step in recovery. To question it must then become his choice."[18] This describes once again that each of us have a choice, but usually everyone has some type of experience where in some way he/she recognizes that there must be a better way. This usually happens when you finally surrender and give up your own way of doing things, recognizing that you were wrong in your thinking, and have the willingness to start questioning, to look deeper for that better way in which the answer will come to you.

In regards to sickness and looking for a cure, if you believed in *only* the following statement, the path to awakening would speed up your learning beyond comprehension, and would keep you healthy and in the light of Joy:

"Only forgiveness heals an unforgiveness, and only an unforgiveness can possibly give rise to sickness of any kind."[19]

CHAPTER 5

EMPOWERING WAYS TO DEAL WITH PAIN

"If God is real, there is no pain.
If pain is real, there is no God."[1]

As I awoke one morning in January of 2017, I remembered a very symbolic dream that I had the night before. In this dream, there was a man jumping on a trampoline, but what was interesting about it was that he kept attempting to jump higher and higher each time, never once stopping. His persistence was impressive, because he never gave up the idea that he could go a little higher, and yet higher, and higher still, and nothing could bring him down. I was an observer in the dream, just noticing his endurance. When I awoke,

I was immediately given the thought to never stop reaching for the highest part of myself, and have faith in the process that if you persevere you will reach new heights, new understanding, and greater awareness that precedes awakening. But you can't give up. There may be obstacles along the way, but you don't have to let them stop you. Just keep jumping, reaching for new heights. In other words, keep your eye on the goal.

You don't have to know what each step will look like on the way nor have any of that figured out. You don't have to be perfect. Just focus on the goal, which is true peace, understanding, and real vision. If this is all you want, then things start showing up that symbol-ize your decision, just as when you decide to be well, things start showing up in your experience that reflect your decision to be well. It's always the decision in the mind that comes first, and the rest takes care of itself. It's important to trust this process without any attach-ment to a particular outcome.

Pain is a mental process, not a physical one

It is precisely this mentality, along with forgiveness, that will help you deal with pain in whatever form it shows up in your life. When dealing with pain, you might want to try thinking of the idea that all pain is a mental process, not a physical one. This is not always easy to think about when you are feeling intense pain in your body, but just entertaining the idea for a while helps you to gain some control over how you feel. If pain is a mental process, not a physical one, then you can use the power of your mind to choose how you are perceiving it, as we discussed in the last chapter.

Many people doing the *Course* get caught in level confusion. The idea that the world and bodies are illusions doesn't mean that you neglect the body. If you are feeling intense pain, it can be very loving to take medication or do what you would normally do to help alleviate it. In your mind you can know and practice the Truth, and at the same time do whatever you feel guided to do without guilt.

Another idea that may be helpful is that pain does not have to equal suffering. In other words, pain may feel physical, but suffering is a choice. You do not have to choose to suffer. This gives you your power back and helps reinforce the idea that you are not powerless when it comes to the body. The attitude that goes along with this is that the body in and of itself has no power because it is an effect, not cause. If the cause of pain and suffering is in your mind, then you can exercise your mind's muscle by practicing a different way of looking at your pain. For starters, it can be an exercise in true forgiveness taking the form of the great line in the workbook of the *Course*, "The guiltless mind cannot suffer."[2] Or, "I am as God Created me. His Son can suffer nothing. And I am His Son."[3]

This is not to say that you shouldn't be normal and take your medication, or whatever it is in form that may be helpful. This is not about giving up any advice from your doctor unless it truly feels uncomfortable to you. Most of us need what the *Course* calls "magic" to help us heal because our minds believe we are bodies that need these "outside agents" that we believe will heal us. Sometimes it is helpful to have a combination approach to help the mind heal without fear. So, you can practice the mind work, and at the same time take medicine, and this may be very helpful. If you practice the understanding that the body is not the cause of healing, even while you take medication, you are helping yourself remember the truth. If you feel intuitively that you don't need to be on medication, and it truly feels inspired, then I believe you can trust that. You will also know by how you feel in general what works for you. There is not one right way of dealing with body pain. It is always recommended to work with your thoughts and practice forgiveness, and if that alone works for you, then great. If you feel it is helpful to do the combination approach that is fine, too. The important thing is how you are thinking about everything.

This chapter will intentionally focus more on things that can be helpful on this physical level where we believe we are. The *Course* is not about denying our bodily experience, but helping ourselves move through this life experience with peace and grace regardless of what is going on with the body. At the same time, we can remember that the body only responds to the thoughts in the mind. I was astounded when I first read the following words in the *Course*: Jesus said, "It is the body that is outside us, and is not our concern."[4] This shows how little he believed in the body to do anything. I was so inspired by this comment! Think about it, and say it a few times to yourself. It states that the body in and of itself is nothing and doesn't do anything because it's a projection coming from the mind, and isn't real. In fact, Jesus also says, "At no single instant does the body exist at all."[5] This may be hard to believe at first, and quite disturbing, because our experiences here in the world tell us something different. We can see, touch, taste, feel and smell; the famous five senses. The ego defines itself by these five senses, as if that is all we are. We are not limited to these five senses, in fact, we are much greater and beyond these senses. We are unlimited beings, full of potential.

These statements about the body not existing negate everything we think we believe. Of course it may appear threatening at first. Somewhere in our minds we know it to be true, that what we are seeing and experiencing is not even there, and this is what is frightening. These same ideas can be truly valuable if used to help you deal with pain, remembering that the body doesn't define you because it isn't who you are. It is just an image.

All pain and illness comes from the unconscious guilt in the mind, whether it's a cold or cancer. This comes from the ego part of the split mind that scripted illness in various forms that was set up at the seeming beginning of time. If you find yourself mentally reviewing a painful part of your script, instead of judging yourself for this, try to be gentle and patient with yourself, and stick with forgiveness, following the steps presented to you in Chapter Two. **Forgiveness leads to peace and the gradual undoing of the ego, the inventor of pain.** You can now practice viewing the script with the Holy Spirit as your teacher as you move through the experience.

Remembering to laugh is also an essential part of remembering the lightness of your Spirit. So, here is a joke for you (good one for us Hollywood folks) and hopefully it won't provide you with a forgiveness opportunity as some of my jokes have innocently done in the past!

A middle aged woman had a heart attack and was taken to the hospital. While on the operating table she had a near death experience. Seeing God she asked "Is my time up?" God answered, "No, you have another 40 years, 2 months and 8 days to live." Upon recovery, the woman decided to stay in the hospital and have a facelift, liposuction, and a tummy tuck. She even had someone come in and change her hair color. Since she had so much more time to live, she thought she might as well make the most of it. After her last operation, she was released from the hospital. While crossing the street on her way home, she was hit by a car and died immediately. Arriving in front of God, she demanded,

"I thought you said I had another 40 years, why didn't you pull me from out of the path of the car?" God replied, "I didn't recognize you."

We live in a world where the idea of having a perfect body is encouraged, and if your body is healthy, some equate that with being spiritual. The answer is not to have a perfect body, rather your reaction to it is what matters. The world and the body are constantly changing, and bodies eventually crumble, as will everything that is not permanent or based on reality. However, you can learn to get in touch with the unchanging, constant peace in your mind that never shifts or changes.

In times when you are having some difficulty with body issues, do the normal thing and take care of it the best you can. **Take it one day at a time, and one thought at a time**. Try to watch your mind wandering, not letting it get out of control with fear thoughts. It may help to remind yourself of the Truth, and repeat to yourself often that you are not a body, but perfect spirit, whole and innocent. Everything that God creates is exactly the same as He is, and therefore He created you perfect.

In order to realize our innocence and perfection as God created us, we need to understand how the ego operates so that we can choose against it. This is one of the empowering ways to deal with pain. The problem is that the ego likes pain because pain is one way the ego proves that it exists apart from God. If pain is present,

God is non-existent. Of course this is unconscious to us and comes from the guilt in the mind from having chosen to be separate from Him. Pain allows the ego to place the cause outside, and therefore render ourselves powerless. Since most of us have identified with the ego, we believe we deserve to suffer as a way of punishing ourselves so God won't punish us Himself. Of course this idea is absurd because God is perfect love and doesn't know Himself to be anything other than Himself. So, love is just itself.

Thinking about pain with the ego is what hurts us. One could feel pain in the body with this attitude, "What does the body have to do with me?" This idea can be practiced in the mind as you are doing whatever you can to take care of yourself and the body. This does not contradict the idea that you are not your body. It's about developing a healthy attitude and way of looking at things while you continue to live a normal life. If you have a choice, why not choose to remember your wholeness despite what is going on in the body? It can truly set you free.

Pain is just another form that illusions take, so it is not special in any way. When the *Course* says that there is no hierarchy of illusions, it means that one illusion is not harder or bigger, or more important or special than another because this whole dream we call the world is one vast illusion. The only thing that matters is which teacher you are viewing your life with, the ego or the Holy Spirit.

In times when you feel overwhelmed or tired of taking care of your body, try practicing not taking it too seriously. I don't mean that you should neglect your body or not do what is helpful for it, but I mean the attitude you have in your mind. Not taking it seriously may sound blasphemous to the ego, but do not listen to your ego. The ego doesn't know anything. The ego, or the world of perception, is not knowledge. Try not to use pain as an obstacle to greater understanding and peace. Guilt and sickness are one and the same, and to release yourself from this the *Course* says that "the insignificance of the body must be an acceptable idea."[6] This takes daily practice because we have all trained ourselves to believe the opposite, that the body is holy, special, and significant. **Practicing healing thoughts when you are overwhelmed with pain can simply take the form of repeating a statement several times to yourself that for you means your innocence. Statements such as "I have no need for this pain." "Let me remember the true purpose of the body." Or simply, "Holy Spirit, help me remember the truth, that I am innocent, whole, and complete."**

We think our life here in the world is real life, but the truth is that in real life you don't die and then are reborn again and again. We do appear to have that experience, but it is still part of the illusion. Real life doesn't shift or change, because it is eternal. Real life is with God in Heaven. Heaven is an awareness of perfect oneness. So, real life is perfect Oneness with God.

It probably seems like it is much easier to think this way when you feel no pain at all. What is challenging is seeing the light when you feel the darkness. It is in these times that it is helpful to develop trust in the process, that when given over to the Holy Spirit, you are being totally taken care of. You can trust that. In fact, if everything went perfectly well in our lives all the time and we never had any challenges to face, and everything was completely forgiven, we'd be in what the *Course* calls the real world, where true peace is experienced all the time. This is possible, and will happen, but most of us aren't there yet, so these obstacles we face are really blessings that help us have the motivation to go within and seek the answers there instead of outside ourselves. This helps shift the purpose of body pain or any illness from the ego's way of looking at it to letting it serve the Holy Spirit's purpose. In the next chapter, I will discuss mental processes that will assist in making this shift from pain (which is a symbol of separation) to joy, representing your true nature as Spirit.

Another way to practice thinking about pain is to think about some of the more difficult or painful experiences in your life. You got through them, didn't you? If you are reading these pages in this book right now, that means you made it through those difficult times to get to where you are right now reading these pages. Sometimes you may even find yourself saying, "How did I get through that?" This is what I have said to myself after that experience I described with anxiety in my 20's. There is a part of your mind that is still in touch with the Holy Spirit, the Christ Mind that knows you as you really are in your wholeness. It is this part that we are in touch with at some level that helps us have the strength to keep going. You can always rely on this because it's a part of you, and you are not separate from this inner strength and wisdom that comes from God. In fact, this is the one thing you truly can count on that will never fail in providing you with comfort when you feel you most need it. God does not leave us comfortless, and this is why the Holy Spirit, also referred to as the Comforter, was given to us as the Voice for God that resides in the right part of our minds. **Choosing the Holy Spirit *is* our remembering of God.** It is the remaining communication link between God and His separated Sons. So, when we choose the Holy Spirit as our teacher at any given moment, we are experiencing a Holy Instant where comfort will indeed be given us. I'd like to share some lyrics with you from one of the songs I wrote on my Awakening to Love CD about the Holy Spirit as being the Great Comforter. It's called "The Comforter." Please let these words sink deeply in your mind, and remember that He is always with you:

The Comforter

Beyond the moon, beyond the stars
Past the beauty of your loving heart
I will be with you for all of time
I'll be the Vision through your eyes

In the calmness of the autumn rain
I will wash away your weary days
And when the morning sun appears
I'll be the warmth to dry your tears

In quiet dreams where you feel alone
I'll be the soft voice that calls you home
When you awaken to the journey's end
I'll reach for you...please take my hand

You can always come back to this quiet place in your mind anytime you choose. It is always there regardless if you are aware of it or not. It is something permanent that you can count on, wholly authentic, and wholly loving. Also, in the midst of severe pain, whether psychological or physical, you can train your mind to remember to come back to that first forgiveness step, identifying the cause that you are dreaming that you have an unhealed mind taking the form of a sick body or mental illness. Perhaps the lesson is coming to you in a physical form to remind you to let go of any investment in seeing yourself as sick. We may not think of ourselves as being invested in sickness, but when we search our minds carefully, we will notice that most of the thoughts we are having center around our illness, and the thoughts are usually representing some form of fear. This is investing in fear. We need to gently turn our attention inward and start actively choosing different thoughts, so that our thoughts reflect the love in our minds instead of fear. **We spend so much time in our outer world,**

that it would be wise to start spending more time in our inner world.

I've spoken a lot about the mind level, and now I want to suggest some practical ways of taking care of oneself at the physical level that can contribute to a sense of well-being. If you are one of the many people that value preventative health care, you may find some of these next ideas to be helpful in maintaining a sense of well-being in general. For more empowering ways to deal with pain at the mind level, I recommend also practicing the exercises you will find in Chapter 6. As I mentioned before, since we believe we are bodies, there are certain things that can help the ego relax, calming it's "raucous shrieks," on the level of the physical.

1. Massage

Massage is a wonderful way of relaxing the ego, and of course as your muscles relax, tension and stress start to slip away. If you are experiencing pain in certain areas of your body, try having someone massage other areas that are not in pain, if possible. Some examples are your feet, hands, scalp, heart, abdominal area, and ears, which are often neglected areas of the body. You can actually massage some of these areas yourself. Many nerves are connected to various organs in the body, and you will feel a sense of warmth and well-being all over when you massage some of these areas, especially the feet, scalp, and ears. I try to get at least one massage a month because I know the great benefits that come from it. Also, your defenses are down which means you will be more receptive and open to the Holy Spirit's guidance.

2. Spending time in nature

Another comforting thing to do that doesn't cost any money and is very practical is to spend more time in nature, especially breathing in the air in a heavily wooded or mountainous setting. Let the sounds in nature become a part of you until you feel you are one with the sounds. Feel the vibrations of the sounds of nature all throughout your body as if you are vibrating as one entity. Allow yourself to be in the space until you feel a deep sense of peace wash over you and through you. This is similar to what I imagined when I was feeling the vibration of my cat's purr move throughout my entire body. It was very healing. Sound is the future of healing. It's already here, but not so popular yet.

3. Walk barefoot on a grassy area

Another very healing and exhilarating thing to do is to walk on a grassy area barefoot. Feel your feet on the ground and imagine the raw, natural energy of the earth move through your feet and up through your body and over the top of your head. Feel a sense of rootedness and centeredness as you do this and imagine the healing, white light of the Holy Spirit surrounding your whole being until it becomes a part of you. Say to yourself, "I am the light of the world,"[7] several times in your mind. Give yourself enough time to be in the space until that same feeling of peace washes over you and through you.

4. Drink plenty of water, some with electrolytes

Try to drink plenty of water, some with hydrating electrolytes such as coconut water. Of course you want to pay attention to your own dietary restrictions, if you have any from your doctor. I personally noticed that when I started taking in more electrolytes such as from coconut water and other sources, my frequent headaches went away. I believe as I made a decision in my mind to be well, the form of that decision showed up in ways that were helpful.

5. Take small, baby steps toward your goals

If you have a goal you are trying to reach, practice taking small steps here and there to reach it. You do not have to overload yourself with too much all at once. For example, in writing this book I tried not to think of all the chapters at once, and what I would say in each chapter. Instead, I focused on one chapter at a time. This helped me not get too overwhelmed by all the work ahead of me. Another example would be if you are trying to lose weight. Practice focusing on small steps you can take each day, such as adjusting one part of your diet. Maybe the next day you will add an exercise. The following day you might do something else to contribute to your goal, such as eating what you want, but in smaller portions. The point is to take it step by step. This will create a momentum in which the small steps start to add up if you are doing them with some consistency. A combination approach to everything is usually helpful: You give up one food item, you cut down on quantity on another, and you add one exercise. This way you will be less likely to take things to extremes and feel deprived. With practice, focus, and discipline, you will do it!

All the specific forms addictions take come from the ego's need to build up and validate itself. All of us are addicted to the ego or we wouldn't appear to be here. **Just as we can change our minds *thought by thought*, we can work on those things we want to improve upon in our daily lives *step by step*.** Also, the more forgiveness is practiced, inspiration will be given you to do what naturally reflects the love in your mind. There is no right or wrong way of doing things. Just practice doing it without guilt.

6. Steps to shift your thinking about pain

1. Keep your eye on the goal of remembering that the pain is in your mind, which means you can change your mind about it. Think of the Holy Spirit, imagining Its Light washing over you and through you, so you become One with the Light. Imagine the Holy Spirit absolving you of all belief in guilt. Its Light is streaming through you with no break or limit anywhere. Practice this until you feel a sense of peace.

2. Let go of attachment to a particular outcome.

3. Trust that all is being taken care of and you are safe and whole in the Light of God. There is nothing more you need do.

All of these ideas are general suggestions to do as an aside to all the mental work that was discussed. An example of how inspiration from forgiveness showed up for me as a symbol of health and well-being was in my decision to take in more plant-based foods filled with natural life force. I felt better in general, and my mood was better. I included eating wild blueberries, raw fruit juices, fresh celery juice, kale, cilantro, and any leafy greens, apples, dates, and whole grains. These are just some examples of things that have helped me maintain a sense of health and well-being on the physical level, as well as having more energy in general, so I am sharing them with you. I cut out most wheat products and most dairy from my diet and I feel a tremendous difference in my physical health. It takes discipline to do these things regularly, but it also depends on how important maintaining a sense of well-being is to you. This is demonstrated by practicing forgiveness at the same time. In fact, practicing forgiveness leads you to all sorts of things that reflect your wanting to be well, and the above suggestions are just some examples of things I am doing that reflect my decision to be well. I recognize they aren't the cause of my being well, but a symbol of that choice. They may resonate with you, or may not. One should always do what feels truly helpful.

I want to point out that in truth we don't even need to follow the laws of nutrition to be well, but as long as we believe we are bodies, it doesn't do much good to deny our experience here as bodies.

When it comes to dietary health, a book that I recommend is "Medical Medium" by Anthony Williams. This book lists some of these foods I suggested plus much more information on various illnesses, and how one can treat them using natural foods and herbs, which are also symbols of the mind's decision to be well. The information comes from Spirit, channeled through this medium. If you are thinking, oh no, another medium, I tried some of the combinations of foods he recommended for various body issues and I can honestly say I have noticed a positive difference in how I feel. I also recommend his other book called "Life-changing Foods." There are some excellent natural recipes in there, including many wonderful juicing varieties.

The ultimate thing to understand is that you are innocent regardless of what you choose to do here in the world, and the most important thing to understand is that whatever you do, practice doing it without guilt. If you have a piece of cake, try eating it without the guilt. My thinking is that as long as we need to eat, we might as well enjoy it! It's much healthier to eat with joy then with guilt. When we eat with guilt, we are eating with the ego, which is just the ego's need to confirm itself. This is the cause of all addictions in general, whether it's overeating, over-drinking, or over-anything. The ego is seeking salvation outside itself in substances, which it thinks is the cause of joy. Salvation has nothing to do with the outside picture. Salvation is the understanding that our Will is One with God's, and that we are already full of His Love, truly abundant as His One Son, all of us together. This process involves undoing the ego thought system so that this understanding of Truth becomes our experience.

7. Joy Exercise (helpful for addictions)

In working with addictions, an exercise to practice is to bring to mind a positive memory that brings you great joy; a feeling of connection to God, and great peace. Now, let go of attachment to the event being the cause, and retain the joy. Let the joy stay with you. Let the feeling of that joy empower you, and wash over you, with the attitude that there is nothing your unlimited-ness cannot do! This reminds your mind that outside sources or substances are not the cause of your joy or comfort. You can practice letting go of the teacher in your mind that led to the abuse (the ego) and choose the teacher of healing (the Holy Spirit). It's an inside job. And…you are worth the consistent effort! With conviction you will succeed!

Our thoughts are very powerful, and all thought produces effects in some form. Whatever we do, if we do it with joy, we are contributing to the well-being of the mind. Everything here in the world is a symbol that reflects the thought of separation in the mind. However, we do not have to use our experience here to reinforce the separation. Instead, our only function is how we are interpreting what our body's eyes see, and whichever interpretation we give something becomes our experience. So, we are always at cause, and are the cause of the world we see. This doesn't mean that you are responsible for other people's behavior. You are indeed responsible for how you interpret another's behavior, or how you choose to think about it. This is the same point I made above regarding how we take care of our bodies. If we interpret the body through the ego, we will always use it in the form of attack; to condemn, judge, and further separate in some form. If the body is interpreted through the Holy Spirit, we will use the body as a communication device to allow the Holy Spirit's love, wisdom, understanding, and compassion to work through us so that we can extend it to our brothers and sisters in Christ.

I would like to close this chapter with the following quote from the *Course*, and some additional thoughts: "Healing is accomplished the instant the sufferer no longer sees any value in pain. Who would choose suffering unless he thought it brought him something, and something of value to him?"[8]

Even if it is unconscious to us, we value pain because pain says that we exist as a body, separate from God. There will usually be resistance to

healing, because we are perceiving the world in a way that gives power to the body as being the decision maker. This is an example of why the *Course* urges us to question every value that we hold. It is a *Course* in thought reversal, where we are learning to *unlearn* our mistakes, which are the mistaken choices we make with the ego. What we all value, the body, is being called into question which is frightening to the ego. Gently, and through loving kindness, we can choose again what we call our identity. Are we One with God, eternal and free, or are we a body, separate from God, and imprisoned by our own thinking? The choice is an easy one to make once we let go of what hurts us, and what is truly valueless, that which keeps us rooted in dreams.

CHAPTER 6

PRACTICAL EXERCISES TO EXPERIENCE MENTAL HEALTH

*"What is the peace of God? No more than this;
the simple understanding that His Will is wholly
without opposite. There is no thought that
contradicts His Will, yet can be true."*[1]

Let us be reminded that health is inner peace. Your true nature as Spirit is already in a state of perfect Health. Since we believe we are separate from this state, we do need to undo the ego and remove the blocks to the awareness of love's presence to experience this reality. So the focus is at the mind level where true change occurs.

When we have peace in the mind, we are in a state of health regardless of what is going on with the body. Sometimes the body gets well, and sometimes it doesn't. But now we know we do not have to judge it either way, understanding that to judge it is to make the body real. All pain, whether psychological or physical is a mental process, not a physical one. This is because ideas do not leave their source, which means that the body has not left the mind. The *Course* says that we are mentally reviewing that which has already gone by, and an important question becomes: Why are we choosing to mentally review this particular script of our lives, which includes pain and suffering? When we remember that we are reviewing a script, there must be a reason why we chose it. A right-minded reason is that there is a tremendous opportunity to use the events in our lives for a different purpose than the ego's, where we do not have to be victims of our chosen scripts. This will help us undo the ego's purpose for our scripts, which is to hide the fact that we have a mind that we can return to and make a different choice about the world and our place in it.

How do we get to this experience of mental health, where the mind is truly at peace? Along with true forgiveness, which does lead to peace, there are various exercises one can do to reinforce right-minded thinking, which helps you to develop the habit of thinking with the Holy Spirit. It is important to practice these everyday. Experiencing the positive benefits of choosing the Holy Spirit as your teacher can be immediate, and doesn't have to take time. The *Course* says, "It has taken time to misguide you so completely, but it takes no time at all to be what you are."[2]

Here are some exercises I recommend for mental health, helping you to stay in your right mind:

1. Put the Holy Spirit in charge of your day

This means that you are not doing anything on your own, or with the ego as your teacher. When you are doing things with the ego, or thinking with the ego, this leads to the feeling of being alone. This is where all forms of loneliness come from; the separation from God, which understandably would produce a sense of lack. It is only this lack that requires correction. So, you might say:

Holy Spirit, please be in charge of my day today, including my thoughts and my actions. I am certain that if I follow you I will experience peace.

Then, just let it go and trust that you are being taken care of, which you are. Sometimes I remind myself at different points throughout the day that the Holy Spirit is in charge. Any time you think of it, say it slowly to yourself. In my husband's book, "The Disappearance of the Universe," Gary's teachers Arten and Pursah say that this is one of the ways of undoing the ego, putting the Holy Spirit in charge of your day. This is simple and easy to do, and doesn't take much time.

I say these words above to myself every single morning
before I get out of bed, and remind myself throughout
the day. It feels good to not be in charge of your day,
but it *is* your responsibility to choose how you are looking at it.

2. Practice True Prayer

True Prayer in the *Course* means "the single voice Creator and creation share; the song the Son sings to the
Father, Who returns the thanks it offers Him unto the
Son."[3] Arten and Pursah in "The Disappearance of the
Universe" also say that this is one of the ways of undoing the ego, and it is offered by the Holy Spirit as a way
of reaching God. True Prayer is not about going to God
and asking for things you think you need. It is about
asking to receive what has already been given you by
God; to accept His gifts as yours. These are true gifts,
and what you really want, whether you know it or not
yet. In joining with God in True Prayer, you are seeking the Kingdom of Heaven first, and then the *Course*
says in the "Song of Prayer" section, "The form of the
answer, if given by God, will suit your need as you see
it. This is merely an echo of the reply of His Voice.
The real sound is always a song of thanksgiving and
of Love.[4] You cannot, then, ask for the echo. It is the
song that is the gift. Along with it come the overtones,
the harmonics, the echoes, but these are secondary. In
true prayer you hear only the song, all the rest is merely
added. You have sought first the Kingdom of Heaven,

and all else has indeed been given you."[5] "All else" means all the specifics we might be concerned about, such as our own safety and health, the well-being of our family members, our pets, and our country.

Joining with God in true prayer is how to receive true inspiration. This is the answer to every question you've ever had about anything. We need to allow ourselves this time with God to develop trust that it is safe to go within, and that what we really seek we already have. This process is a way of remembering God, our true Source.

If you get into the habit of practicing true prayer on a daily basis, you will experience great benefits, and a peace and calmness will more readily flow through you. I have had some profound results in practicing true prayer in the form of inspired guidance coming to me through an idea that pops into my mind. The feeling that came with this is that I didn't think the thought. It was just given to me, and required no effort at all. That is the Holy Spirit. Also, if it is inspired the idea will feel good to you precisely because it speaks for God, and it represents the Truth. You will recognize this Truth when you hear it because it is undeniable.

I've put Arten and Pursah's words from the chapter in "The Disappearance of the Universe" on **True Prayer and Abundance** into five specific steps to make it easier to follow:

1. Visualize taking the Holy Spirit or Jesus's hand and going to God

2. Lay your problems and goals, and idols on the altar before God as gifts

3. Think of how much you love Him and how grateful you are to be taken care of, forever safe and totally provided for.

4. Then, become silent with the attitude that God created you to be exactly the same as He is, and He wants you to be with Him forever.

5. Now, let go and join with God's love and lose yourself in joyful communion with Him.[6]

So, the idea is that when you empty your mind of your perceived desires, you can experience God's love, His true gift. Later, when you least expect it, you may receive inspired guidance which can come through a dream, an inspired idea in your mind, a song, or in any other form. Be open to receiving and stay tuned in. The form will show up that will be truly helpful to you. The Holy Spirit knows what that is, and our job is to trust it. The *Course* explains that when we join with God first, we've been given the answer. The answer is already within you, but you only need to accept it.

Arten and Pursah go on to explain that God's answers are an internal process, not an external one. If something shows up in the world it is always a symbol, but can show up as symbols of safety or abundance. This is the power of this exercise! The true gifts from God that the *Course* speaks of are naturally yours, and you don't have to earn them; things like love, sinlessness, perfection, knowledge and eternal truth. You are already worthy, and do not have to prove it or earn it. There may be resistance to practicing true prayer because the ego doesn't want to join with God. It wants to remain a special, individual self. The ego shows its resistance by statements such as "I don't have time to do it. I'll do it later. I'll do it tomorrow." I always try to remember this idea: I have so much time during the day to do all these other things, so if I can't set aside five minutes of time to join with God, that must mean that I'm placing more importance on something else. It just comes down to willingness.

Before I get to the next exercise, I'd like to reiterate that if the goal of the *Course* is true peace, then it is in practicing these methods as often as possible that you will attain the goal. For most of us, we say we want the goal faster. What helps us to achieve this goal faster is our willingness to practice the steps we've been given. And the more we practice, the more we start to form new habits in our thinking where it becomes our natural way of being as part of having a forgiving attitude.

3. Practice the Rules For Decision in the *Course* in Chapter 30

The Rules for Decision is one of the most powerful summaries of how you can spend your day in peace.

Jesus guides you step by step in how to start your day on a right-minded note. I won't go through each step in specific detail since it is lengthy, but I recommend reading this section in the *Course* to get the essence of what he is saying. In a nutshell, he is teaching us that we are making decisions all the time without realizing we are making them. He is helping us gain some control over our thoughts so we can stay on a right-minded track. This entails letting go of being our own judge of what to say or do, judging on our own how we should respond to situations, because when we judge them on our own, we have already set the stage for how it is going to play out, which will produce fear about being open to another way.

This is precisely what appeared to happen at the beginning of the separation. We decided on our own that we wanted to be a special and individual self, apart from God, which did set the stage as we wanted it to be, hence the world we see now. We relive the separation in many forms over and over until we realize we can change our minds and think differently.

Jesus is also telling us that the clarification of the goal belongs at the beginning. We can decide the kind of day we want to have, and keep that goal in our minds throughout the day. When we forget our goal and start judging, which is inevitable at times, we can undo our judgment by reminding ourselves that we can go back into the mind and have the openness for another answer that will work for us. If there is resistance to being open, this means you have judged on your own. This is when you want to let go of the need to be right, and admit you lost sight of the goal and forgot what it is, which cancels out your previous error of judging on your own.

If you still find there is resistance to changing your mind, Jesus says follow that up with "At least I can decide I do not like the way I feel now."[7] Then you can say, "And so I hope I've been wrong."[8] This is helpful in that it is a reminder that you are not being forced into anything, but help is something that you want. You will start to trust that you will benefit from being wrong when you are open to another way of seeing. Now, you can say with honesty "I want another way to look at this."[9] It is at this point when you remember what it is you really want. And the final follow up is "Perhaps there is another way to look at this. What can I lose by asking?"[10]

Again, I am only paraphrasing the details of these steps, but this gives you the idea of what it means to take things thought by thought when you feel you have already spiraled downward into negativity. If you recall, at the beginning of Chapter Two, I discussed the thought form I received from the Holy Spirit encouraging us to take it thought by thought when you find strong resistance to changing your mind. This process is very important. Please refer to the "Rules for Decision" section of Chapter 30 in the *Course* for a more extended commentary on each step.

I practice these "Rules for Decision" in my own life. They are very helpful, not only as a detailed practical way to train us in right-minded thinking, but because it's a reminder that our days are not happening randomly. We decide to set it up for ourselves by who we are perceiving our day with, the ego or the Holy Spirit.

4. Exercise in becoming aware of the Light of Truth in you (You are indeed the Light of the World!)

Even in intense trauma, you can become aware of your thoughts. It is the judgments you are holding in the form of grievances that block the light of truth in you.

Close your eyes and take some time and search your mind, looking at each attack thought, saying to yourself that this thought is blocking me from experiencing the love of God, and from practicing my true function of forgiveness. Remember that no matter how intense the situation may be, the quiet center of your mind where the Holy Spirit resides is still present within you. Seek to find it. Be active in not letting your mind wander or slip away. Let the body slip away from your awareness. The body is not you. Say to yourself slowly and with conviction, "I am the light of the world. Holy Spirit, help me to remove the blocks to the awareness of love's presence, so I can experience that I am the Light of the world."

Let the following words sink deep into your mind: Forgiveness looks past the dark clouds of guilt to the

Light that shines within you. Your purpose is not found in all the dark forms illusions take; rather it's beyond them, because you share your purpose with God, that you be exactly the same as He is. Purpose in any real sense is Joy. When you are aligned with purpose, you serve as the Light of the world, reminding others of their Light, while reinforcing that Light within yourself, and that is very joyful.

Imagine taking Jesus's hand and walking with Him through the darkness, whatever form it takes. You can be certain that he is with you. See that when you walk with Him, your fear thoughts have no substance and cannot stop you from reaching the Light. With conviction you will succeed. The outcome of Love is certain regardless of the beliefs you hold about yourself or others. You cannot truly lose yourself, because no matter how much you idolize illusions and make them your reality, you are still part of God, and have never truly separated. This keeps you safe. Although you can elect to choose to divide yourself and hide the Light in you, you cannot obliterate the Light because the Light represents the Truth about you and the Truth cannot be changed.

Let these ideas sink into your mind and imagine you are being breathed by God. You are a thought in the Mind of God, and he is breathing you. Feel gratitude for this greater joining, feeling blessed that only love is real.

5. Exercise in facing fear

Think of fear and any emotion that is a shadow of fear (anxiety, anger, sadness, worry, etc) like a door in your mind. What is fueling the fear is behind the door. It must be attracting you or you wouldn't feel it. Approach the door calmly with love and open it. Don't judge or analyze what's behind the door, rather notice and look at it. See what it is showing you, knowing it can't hurt you because you are not keeping it hidden, but bringing it to the Light. What is the purpose you are using it for? Don't then slam the door on it in anger which makes it real. Gently acknowledge the fear and the purpose it has served without judgment, then let that purpose go while gently closing the door behind you. Open a new door that contains the answer to fear, the answer to separation; the door of the Holy Spirit. Invite Him in to sit with you a while. This is a true friend because He only sees you as you are in Truth, and that is why you can trust Him. It is through Him that your mind will be restored to wholeness. Listen to what He has to say.

6. A Closing Prayer

Close your eyes, and allow yourself to relax, letting the body slip away from your awareness. The body is not you. Say this prayer in your mind, "I am the Son of God, forever whole and innocent. Holy Spirit, help me to remove the blocks to the awareness of love's presence, and recognize that God's love is all that I want.

Help me to overlook the errors I see in other people and in myself, and to see the Holy Son of God in its place. My will is forever One with God. Let me be willing to receive His Will, which is love, and is total and complete. There is nothing else to seek."

"Help me to realize that I am the Light of the world, that I may be a demonstration for Joy and Peace. As I let my own Light shine, it gives others permission to do the same. I am One with God, and I am truly blessed as His Holy Son. Help me to remember this in times of pain, uncertainty and fatigue; that I may remember that I am complete in God's love, and that I am not forgotten."

"I give thanks in love and gratitude, that only love is real. God Is. Amen."

You can mix up these six exercises however you wish, but I recommend that the first three be practiced every day. Let the benefits reveal themselves to you. Your experience will show you that they work. All of these exercises are more helpful if they are done in conjunction with true forgiveness, and not used as a substitute for true forgiveness. The true freedom that comes from true forgiveness will reveal itself to you in pleasant and surprising ways. For example, there may be a situation that always triggers you, and one day the same thing happens and you don't feel disturbed at all. You are at peace. This is a sign that unconscious guilt is being removed from your mind.

Gratitude

Another principle that is very powerful to practice is gratitude, but not the kind of gratitude as the world usually defines it. The world usually thinks of gratitude with the attitude that you should be grateful because you are not suffering like others suffer. Or, you should be grateful and eat all the food on your plate because there are children starving in Africa. You get the idea. People have good intentions with this kind of gratitude, but this is the kind of gratitude that comes from a misperception of the world; seeing oneself as different and separate from another. Whether we appear to be better off or not, we are the same because we share the same mind.

After reading the *Course's* view on gratitude, I was very humbled by it. Lesson 195 says: "Love is the way I walk in gratitude." Jesus says, "For who has cause for thanks while others have less cause? And who could suffer less because he sees another suffer more?"[11]

He continues, "It is insane to offer thanks because of suffering."[12] Jesus is again raising the bar. Gratitude is only authentic when it is joined in Love, making no comparisons of any kind. Making comparisons is another ego device for separation. It's a trick. Jesus is asking us to be sincere in our gratitude by making it all inclusive, that we are all on this path together. If our thinking is that we are not walking together as one, then we are not really getting anywhere. We must see ourselves as unified with everyone. And finally, with this attitude comes the idea that "We rejoice that no exceptions ever can be made which would reduce our wholeness, nor impair or change our function to complete the One Who is Himself completion. We give thanks for every living thing, for otherwise we offer thanks for nothing, and we fail to recognize the gifts of God to us."[13]

I wrote a song called "Gratitude," another song on my CD, *Awakening to Love*. I think the lyrics are relevant here as they reinforce the idea of gratitude being about joining and oneness:

Gratitude, gratitude carries me through
Gratitude keeps my heart closer to you
Gratitude, gratitude a longing for Truth
Gratitude is the way I walk with you
Father I thank you for shining your Light
Remaining perfect Love despite the ego's fight
Forgiveness is the business of the awakening game
From our illusions and delusions that keep us from
  choosing again
Gratitude, gratitude carries me through
Gratitude keeps my heart closer to you
Gratitude, gratitude a longing for Truth
Gratitude is the way I walk with you
Miracles come to the quiet Mind

Resting gently when the moment is right
Leaving no trace of limits behind
Love is the way I remember your strength
In your innocence all my ignorance is melting away
Freedom from the dream of a sleeping mind
A Blessing to behold for us prisoners of time
Gratitude, gratitude carries me through
Gratitude keeps my heart closer to you
Gratitude, gratitude a longing for Truth
Gratitude is the way I walk with you
Love love love is enough
All we need is love love love is enough
All we need is love.

Spirit is always in a state of health because Spirit, what you really are, represents Truth. So in reality you are already perfect, whole and complete. On the physical level, where we believe we are, we need to go through this undoing of the ego, achieving a state of mental health, so that we are preparing ourselves for a higher life form. In the meantime, we can learn to experience the happy dream and the real world, which precedes our awakening in God.

Spirit is in a state of grace forever.
Your reality is only Spirit.
Therefore you are in a state of grace forever.[14]

CHAPTER 7

CHANGE YOUR
MIND, WAKE UP
TO YOUR LIFE

*The images you make cannot prevail against
what God Himself would have you be. Be never fearful of temptation, then, but see it as it is;
another chance to choose again, and let Christ's
strength prevail in every circumstance and every
place you raised an image of yourself before.*[1]

We are now at the place where we can clearly see that
the Mind is the mechanism for change. In fact, Jesus
defines "mind" in the "Clarification of Terms" at the
end of the "Manual for Teachers," saying: "The term
mind is used to represent the activating agent of spirit,

supplying its creative energy." As you learn to give back to the mind its proper role in being the cause of everything you see and experience, you can see any challenge or temptation that comes up as an opportunity to reinforce the strength of Christ in you by choosing to identify with that part of your mind instead of the ego. The more you identify with yourself as Spirit, and practice forgiveness, the more you are chipping away layers of guilt in the unconscious mind. You are then becoming more of what you really are, and are therefore waking up to the awareness of your *real* life as Spirit, One with God. To wake up to your *real* life is to remember that you are dreaming a dream of separation, and if you can accept that you are dreaming, the natural course from there is to wake up. All of the exercises and ideas discussed so far in this book will help you awaken if you practice them and allow them to become part you.

I cannot emphasize enough the helpfulness and importance of doing the Workbook of the *Course* if that is your chosen path. I want to reiterate again that this book is not to be a substitute for the *Course* itself. If you find the information in this book helpful, then it is serving a wonderful purpose; to help a few more find their way by reinforcing the non-dualistic thought system of the *Course* itself.

The closest we can get to real life on the level of the world is when we start experiencing what the *Course* calls the *real* world. This comes from choosing the Holy Spirit over many years, thus practicing right-minded thinking and true forgiveness on a consistent basis. This dedication and consistency of focus is how you become a master.

The *real* world is not to be confused with *real* life. The *Course* says that "There is no life outside of Heaven. Where God created life, there life must be. In any state apart from Heaven life is illusion."[2] So, obviously, anything having to do with the world is not real life. Remember, real life is permanent and never shifts or changes, and nothing appears to die. It is awareness of perfect oneness. When the *Course* is talking about the *real* world, it's talking about what we will experience when all has been forgiven, and all judgment has been relinquished. We will be seeing everything with true perception, which is the highest level of consciousness one can attain. It is not to be confused with knowledge, because the level of perception is not knowledge. If we perceive anything we cannot really *know* God because the level of perception is not knowledge, which is of God. But, we can let what we perceive serve a right-minded purpose, and when we are in the real world, the top of the ladder, we are just beyond the gates of Heaven, meaning that we have become totally identified with the Christ as our nature. Then, God Himself takes the final step and lifts us up unto Himself. There is no way we can possibly understand this at this physical level where we believe we are. The only way to understand it is to experience it, and all of us will come to that experience when we are ready. This statement that "God leans to us and lifts us up, taking salvation's final step Himself"[3] is to be taken as metaphor in the sense that God does not have hands, and is not going to literally lift our bodies up. But we can trust the truth behind the metaphor which is that we are being totally taken care of regardless if we understand the specifics or not.

It is possible to experience revelation, and have a glimpse of what reality is really like. These experiences are temporary and under the guidance of the Holy Spirit. The Holy Spirit knows the revelation readiness of everyone. You can trust that process. I've had many experiences of intense peace that last for just a few seconds, some longer. I'm not saying this was revelation, but I definitely experienced a kind of peace that is not of this world. It's actually difficult to describe. The closest I can come to describing what this is like is that it is a euphoric feeling of well-being; way beyond what sex could offer because it has nothing to do with the body and the pleasures of the body. The love that I felt was so pure, whole and complete. If this is even close to what we will all feel when we awaken in God's love then we are all going to experience an incredible, spiritual, eternal high!

Until we change our minds about what we are, most of us will confuse love with sacrifice. We will continue to choose against the Love of God, thinking that if we choose God's Love we will lose something. Actually, that "something" we fear losing is our ego; the special and individual personality we have become identified with. The *Course* says the exact opposite. It says by choosing God's Love, you lose nothing, but gain everything. **The more love you have in your mind, the less you will feel you are sacrificing**. This reminds me of the beautiful line in the song, "Amazing Grace," "I was blind, but now I see." This idea of choosing God's love is a difficult idea to trust as of yet, because we have become so invested in the world and our personalities as our identity. When we don't value ourselves as children of God, we are giving up our divinity and choosing idols in its place, an insane sacrifice. But as we learn to value spirit over the ego, we start to realize how much we have allowed ourselves to play small, and we actually have been sacrificing our happiness on behalf of something that ultimately brings us pain.

It's lack of mindfulness that contributes to this confusion between love and sacrifice. It is like we are running on thin ice, and we will fall before we've had a chance to rise if we aren't staying mindful throughout the day. Staying mindful means throwing away our childish toys (all the judgments and idols we make of this world) and asking ourselves, "What do I really want and value?" As we continue to practice forgiveness, a natural process unfolds where we start recognizing that what is valuable are those things that help us awaken from the dream. Forgiveness is valuable in that sense. God never forgives because God never condemns. His attitude is simply perfect love from the beginning. We, however, need forgiveness to undo the false sense of self that we made up that we begin to realize has no value.

What is valueless are those things that tempt us to reinforce the dream of separation. The ego thinks in terms of material things that are valuable, and that is because it equates itself with the world and the body. The body is the ego's home, and therefore it will do anything to defend it. The *Course* says, "If I defend myself I am attacked."[4] This idea is meant to be practiced at the mind level, not the physical. For example, if you are walking down the street, and someone tries to hurt you, do whatever is necessary to keep yourself from getting hurt. Do not just stand there and say, "If I defend myself I am attacked." In that kind of situation, what is most loving is to protect yourself and do your best to get out of harm's way. At the mind level, when you get the chance, you can practice the idea that in reality what you really are (perfect spirit) can never be attacked, and that in truth there is no need for defense. This can become part of the attitude of forgiveness, and again is done at the level of the mind, not the body.

From the beginning of time when we chose the separation over our oneness with God, we have projected our fears onto God, feeling like we took His Love away, and now He wants it back. That is a projection of our fear of being separate from His love, and placing it onto God, thinking that He is now going to get revenge. It's understandable now that we all have become confused and rattled, and unstable in our thinking. We are like vicious animals, wanting our feed because we feel attacked and deprived. The ego gives love only to take it away again. It feels it won the greatest prize, usurping God's throne by thinking it created itself. This was the beginning of fear. The *Course* sums it up this way: "Each day, and every minute in each day, and every instant that each minute holds, you but relive the single instant when the time of terror took the place of love."[5]

The Importance of Laughter

This is intense stuff because the ego is not light. It can feel heavy at times, and that is why humor is a very important thing to incorporate in your daily life. The *Course* says, "Into eternity, where all is one, there crept a tiny, mad idea, at which the Son of God remembered not to laugh. In his forgetting did the thought become a serious idea, and possible of both accomplishment and real effects. Together, we can laugh them both away, and understand that time cannot intrude upon eternity."[6] So, by practicing not taking our personal lives and the world too seriously, we can lighten up a bit and remember that the world is worthy of laughter, not tears. We can change our minds by remembering to laugh as we notice ourselves getting too serious about various issues. This is another powerful practice to incorporate into your daily life. Find ways to bring comic relief, watch funny movies, laughing at the silliness of our seriousness. This doesn't mean laughing at another's expense, only the silliness of taking this world too seriously where we start losing our peace. Gary and I do our best to balance out the movies we watch, always trying to include comedies in our repertoire. I always know when I've become unbalanced in my movie watching! I feel it, so I change it up a bit.

In the chaos of public reaction to the Presidential election of 2017, I noticed some creative and humorous signs from protesters. Regardless of one's political position, they provide comic relief:

Signs from protesters:

"I have seen better cabinets at IKEA."

"I cannot believe I still have to protest this shit."

"Respect my existence or expect my resistance."

Regarding protesting, aren't we all protesting various things in our minds every day? We decide first that there is something we don't like, and then because it is upsetting, that idea gets projected out onto the world where too often we then blame the world for our upset. This is an example of level confusion. If the mind decides that the *world* is the problem, then you are a victim of the world you see. If the mind decides that the cause is the choice for the ego in the mind, then you are *not* a victim of the world you see, but the cause of it, meaning you are responsible for how you are thinking about the world. It always comes back to this basic idea of cause being in the mind. This is not to say that you shouldn't speak your mind, or protest something if that is what you are guided to do. Protests can come from love, and with a peaceful goal. So there is nothing wrong with taking action, but it can be inspired action, with a loving purpose. It can make all the difference in your experience of an event.

Have you ever laughed so hard you can't breathe? Have you ever had a giggle fit and can't stop? This is one of the healthiest things that can possibly happen. Usually when this happens it means you are letting go of resistance. You are releasing pent-up feelings and emotions. Letting out this resistance in the form of this kind of laughter is very healing. It almost feels like you just exercised! Edgar Cayce, known as the "sleeping prophet," once said, "Laugh in the most extreme circumstance." He was onto something. As most of us have heard, "laughter is the best medicine." This makes sense when the *Course* itself says that we appeared to get into this insane situation of the world because we took the idea of separation from God seriously and forgot to laugh. So, it is clear that laughter is something that has been forgotten, and can remind you of your true nature as you incorporate more of it into your everyday life.

Speaking of giggle fits, when Gary and I were leading a workshop in Japan in the early part of 2017, I was speaking about how I came to find the *Course* and how I met Gary, and I started to get the giggles. I was having a complete "laugh attack" and I couldn't stop! This went on for five minutes! Every time I tried to continue with my story I could barely get the words out I was laughing so hard. The audience found it so amusing and they were laughing with me, as laughter is contagious. That has never happened to me in a workshop setting before, and it was actually quite refreshing! I was releasing and just letting go of any pent up feelings and emotion and it felt like I had just exercised! Doesn't it feel that way sometimes when we laugh so hard? It's like an exercise in well-being, allowing oneself to completely let go and surrender. This is what I notice when I laugh like that…all defenses are down. There is no fear. Fear cannot come where laughter and joy are present, just as fear cannot intrude upon reality and exist where love is present. **Letting go of seriousness is healing.**

Enlightenment

Waking up to your *real* life starts with all of these various ways that have been discussed so far in the practice of changing your mind. When Jesus became enlightened and awakened in God, we were there with Him. This is possible because the separation from God never really occurred, and we are all still in the mind of God, which we have never left. That is why we were there with Jesus when he became enlightened and woke up. Since most of us still believe we are in bodies living in a world of time and space, we still need to go through the experience of waking up until the ego is undone. Speaking of enlightenment, there are many spiritually advanced souls who still get sick. This doesn't mean they are not enlightened. Enlightenment has nothing to do with the body, rather it is a recognition; a change of mind. Everyone has to appear to leave this world in one way or another. The way someone chooses to leave shouldn't be used to determine his/her level of advancement.

Ultimately, we must accept the Atonement for ourselves, which is remembering that nothing happened because the separation has not occurred, and that is why we are innocent. This can be difficult to accept because everything we've been taught about the world says that it's our reality, and that energy itself is real. Arten and Pursah describe energy as miscreated thought. Because it can shift and change means it's not real. The ego wants what it made to be real, including its own story of creation. Creation is of God, and what He creates is exactly the same as He is. We can withdraw our trust in the ego and place it in God, which is true strength, and completely trustworthy. Someone once said, "Do not trust atoms…they make up everything."

When the ego is undone, we will automatically understand that we have only been dreaming, and that this dream is not our reality. The dream will appear to disappear, and there will be nothing left to miss. This is why my husband Gary's book is called "The Disappearance of the Universe." The universe will appear to disappear when the whole mind is returned to a condition of peace. You will not be separate from anyone or anything. You will not be walking alone and separate in a world where there are separate buildings, and borders, and all of the thousands of forms separation takes. You will recognize your Oneness with everything, which is your Oneness with God. You will realize that you are really giving up nothing in exchange for everything, and this will be all that you want. That decision can start *now;* the decision that you want peace above all else; that you no longer need to be right, but want happiness instead. All of the gifts of God, including His peace, love, and joy are yours to accept here and now. You do not need to wait or delay your happiness any longer. Jesus says, "Every minute and every second gives you a chance to save yourself. Do not lose these chances, not because they will not return, but because the delay of joy is needless."[7]

One of my favorite quotes in the entire *Course* is: "How else can you find joy in a joyless place except by realizing that you are not there."[8] We are never really anywhere except in the Mind of God. My sister, Jackie, and I quote this to each other quite often. We remind each other of the Truth whatever is going on. For example, we both have had jobs that were less than satisfying. We would often call each other at work and inspire each other to remember the Truth. If I was having a challenging day, she would say, "Remember, only love is real." And I would call her on her more challenging days as well with the same message. We would always quote the quote above to each other, reminding ourselves we are not really here, but experiencing everything in the mind. That really helped. It's always a good idea to keep these ideas fresh in the mind because the ego's voice is very loud and always speaks first. Repetition is absolutely essential to progressing along any spiritual path.

Many people have asked about enlightenment in our workshops. The *Course* explains enlightenment as "a recognition, not a change at all."[9] This means that the world may or may not appear to change, but your mind's perception about the world changes. You recognize that you share One Will with God; your purpose has become united. It is the recognition that you have no separate interests, nor a "special" self, different and apart from others. You are One Mind, One with God. Jesus also says, "To be egocentric is to be dis-spirited, but to be Self-centered in the right sense is to be inspired or in spirit. The truly inspired are enlightened and cannot abide in darkness."[10]

When I spoke of the real world earlier, or the forgiven world, that is when you have truly reached the state of enlightenment; when you have become totally identified with your Christ nature. When Jesus reached this stage, he listened to only one voice, the Voice of the Holy Spirit. When you reach this point, you have awakened from the dream, and you may have one foot in the door and one out, but just enough in the door that you can function here. You can be enlightened and still appear to be here in the world. If that is the case, you can be sure that your release from the world will be closely upon you. You will delight in the certainty of knowing your Oneness and accepting the gentle release of the body once and for all, where the quiet choice of letting go of dreams for the final time becomes your reality.

Purpose

Although the *Course* is done at the level of the Mind, not the body, and it is not about behavior or what you do in the world, it is important to understand that this doesn't mean you won't do things in the world, or take action. To be passive means to be passive to the ego thought system. You will always do things, but it can be helpful to remember that what you do comes from what you think. That is the reason to invite the Holy Spirit into your mind every morning to help you remember that purpose is everything. When you get clear on what the purpose is behind anything you do, it will lay the foundation for what you will experience. If it serves a right minded purpose, it will have true meaning. When I think of my purpose, I let go of the world's purpose and replace it with this: "My purpose is to recognize my Holiness and extend it to all my brothers, which is accepting that we are all the same and equal in God." When you are following this spiritual purpose, whatever your chosen path or career in the world will reflect this, and you are giving a wonderful gift to everyone. **It doesn't matter what you do in the world; what matters is the purpose it is serving.**

Whenever I have what feels like a difficult decision to make, I always ask myself, "What is the purpose of this? What is it for?" If I am fearful of confrontation in some form, I ask myself, "What do I want to come of this conversation?" before I speak to the person. What is my goal? What am I trying to reach him/her for? This really helps in setting the tone ahead of time, and puts you in a right-minded frame of mind before you set out to do anything. It is more likely that you will achieve an outcome that you want and that serves everyone, for the highest good of all concerned. In other words, it is about shared interests, and you will be serving your highest and best interests. The *your* in this statement means the larger you, the one mind that we all share; the part of the one mind that is the decision maker; the part of the mind that decides. That is the "you" that Jesus is addressing in the *Course,* not the personality. With *true* forgiveness you are also serving your highest and best interest because it applies to everyone, to all of us as One Mind.

In doing the forgiveness process, Jesus asks us to go back to the very beginning when we as God's Son appeared to make that mistaken choice for separation, remembering that the correction was given for that mistake as well in that very instant. Then choose again your Oneness with God and accept it into your Mind *now.* The present is all there is. This Oneness includes all the people you think you are forgiving. Accept their innocence as your innocence. Every time you do this, you are being born again, re-joining with the Christ that is you.

Getting back to purpose, when purpose is not invited into a situation, the situation has no meaning. The ego will automatically speak first as it usually does, and then the outcome will reflect that choice. **What gives meaning to anything is the purpose it serves, but giving it to the Holy Spirit will give it true meaning**. This is why it can make all the difference in your experience which purpose you are letting something serve, the ego's or the Holy Spirit's.

We still believe we are an individual self, and that is understandable. To repeat an important point, the *Course* will be easier to understand and practice when it is recognized that Jesus is addressing all of us as one mind, not as individual bodies. Since we believe we are bodies, he does use language and metaphor as a way of helping us understand the teachings. Therefore, when true forgiveness is practiced with the idea that you are ONE mind, and not a separate body, it will make more sense. You will get the fact that this is why you are innocent, and why when you think judgmental thoughts about other people, you are hurting yourself. If you see another person as innocent, then *you* are innocent. If you see another as guilty, then *you* are guilty. If there is only one of us, then it would have to follow that whatever we do to another we do to ourselves.

We are always in a state of either accepting or rejecting peace. If you truly want peace above all else, in addition to practicing forgiveness, this entails giving up your own ideas of what everything is for, and allowing another interpretation to take its place. We limit ourselves and others when we project our own ideas of what something means, and therefore cannot let the real purpose of it be shown to us. As we continue to work with changing our minds when we find ourselves caught in an ego trap, the truth will be revealed to us. Instead of looking upon a vengeful world, we will see only beauty, because its purpose has changed. **The temptation to use the images we perceive for our own purposes is a trick of the ego into persuading us we are bodies, weak and frail, and with no escape. It is also the cause of all upset.**

A Blessing

An example: Here is one of the ways the ego tries to trick me into believing I am a body, but also how I use forgiveness in these circumstances. Having to do with animals, this represents one of my most challenging forgiveness lessons throughout my life. A while back I went into a pet store to pick up some cat food for Luna. As usual, I always walk by the cages where they keep the cats and dogs, waiting to be adopted. Almost every time I walk by these cages, I have a thought in some form, even if it's subtle, that these animals should not be locked up in cages, and that they are suffering. This time, as I walked by the cages, I noticed this one particular cat; a beautiful, pure, white cat with loving eyes, just watching all the activities. My thought was, "What a beautiful, sweet, adorable and loving cat. I wish I could adopt him, but I know Luna will not like it, since it's clear she wants to be an "only cat." Then, I started feeling bad for the cat that it was in a cage, and that it must be feeling like it wants to be free, and maybe it feels alone and not cared for. As I was leaving the store, I caught myself. I reminded myself I was projecting my own thoughts onto the cat and assuming that cats also think like humans. How do I know what the cat is thinking? It's very possible he was amused by what he was seeing and in no way suffering in any form. So, I continued to think right-minded thoughts remembering that I was dreaming, and I forgave my projected images and myself for dreaming them. I turned it over to the Holy Spirit, trusting in His strength, that His strength in me will prevail, not these ego thoughts that weren't contributing anything helpful to the situation. I remembered that if I choose to see the cat as suffering, then I suffer as well. Then, I let it go. But something happened later, and this is what can happen as a result of forgiveness. You can receive inspired thoughts and ideas.

Later that day I was at home sitting in a chair, and a thought came into my mind which I knew to be the Holy Spirit because it was just given to me: "How do you know that the cat wasn't blessing *you*?" In other words, offering me a chance to choose again and perceive another situation where God's gifts become my own. I had been thinking of the situation in terms of my own blessing onto the cat (a form of specialness) but wasn't perceiving the cat as simultaneously giving *me* a blessing. Wow! This completely helped me do a 180 in my thinking. Blessings are reciprocal in nature. When we bless, we are blessed in return. As we use what seems like painful situations as a way of thinking about others blessing us, because it gives us the opportunity to choose again how we are thinking about things, the gift becomes ours. Aside from that, ultimately there is no cat because there is no world. Images are not reality. This doesn't mean if you see abuse you allow it to continue; it just means that in your mind you can always come back to the truth, and that is what is helpful. Before I engage in any activity now where my help is sought, or even when I am just starting my day, after I turn it over to the Holy Spirit, I remind myself always that my goal is to be truly helpful. Then I let it go and trust in the process.

The *Course* often talks about "specialness" and the various forms it takes. Whenever we think of ourselves as the "blessed" ones as opposed to others who suffer, and we feel a need to fix something or someone, even judging that we know how to fix it, we have moved into a form of specialness. The goal of specialness is always to separate and make oneself different than another, or better off than another. Specialness says, "You have a problem, and I am going to fix you." What does this do except reinforce the separation, which is based on differences? You are the sick one and I am the healthy one. The *Course* teaches us that we are all the same because we share the same mind, which means we all share the ego thought system, the Holy Spirit's presence, as well as a decision maker that chooses between the two. This is why we are the same. The ego tricks us into focusing only on our differences because the ego is based on separation and differences. Once again, this is not reality, and not who we really are, so we can withdraw our belief in it. We do not have to fear the ego because we made it by our belief in it, which means we can withdraw our belief in it.

Changing our minds and waking up to our real life with God requires that first step, that is, the invitation to Spirit that says, "There must be a better way." Then, determination and willingness must follow to seek it out and make it a part of your everyday life. Then you can start living from a place of cause, letting go of all the effects of the world's mistakes. **God's Holiness is yours. Once this is finally accepted, health and well-being are yours forever.**

ABOUT THE AUTHOR

Cindy Lora-Renard is an international speaker on *A Course in Miracles*, as well as a spiritual life coach, with a Master's Degree in Spiritual Psychology from the University of Santa Monica. She has been traveling the world with her husband, Gary R. Renard, in addition to her solo events, helping to introduce the teachings of *A Course in Miracles* to many countries. Cindy participates in the workshops through speaking, singing and guiding meditations.

Cindy is also an accomplished singer/songwriter. In her music, she blends an eclectic mix of New Age, and Alternative Pop with a Celtic flavor, as well as meditative sounds to create a unique style. Cindy uses her knowledge of *A Course in Miracles*, as well as in music and psychology, as "healing" tools to help others awaken into the "higher" octaves of life.

Cindy was born in Toledo, Ohio, to two very educated and accomplished teachers. Her father, Ron Lora (now in retirement) is an award winning History professor who taught at the University of Toledo in Ohio. Her mother, Doris Lora (now in retirement) was a highly respected Music professor at the same University, who later changed careers and received her Ph.D in Psychology. Both continue to remain very active in their communities.

When Cindy was 17 she moved out to Los Angeles, CA. with her mother where she still resides. She started on a spiritual path in her early 20's, going through the spiritual buffet line until she encountered *A Course in Miracles*, which became her chosen path. She eventually met and fell in love with her husband, Gary Renard, a prominent teacher of *A Course in Miracles*, and best-selling author of several books of his own. A gradual process unfolded where Cindy realized the direction her path was meant to take. She continues to enjoy her work as a speaker, spiritual life coach, and singer, and meeting people from all over the world. She likes to say, "We are all in this together."

KEY TO REFERENCES

As a key to footnotes and references, please follow the examples below of the numbering system used for *A Course in Miracles*. Other resources quoted from are also noted below.

T-26.IV.4:7. = Text, Chapter 26, Section IV, Paragraph 4, Sentence 7.

W-pI.169.5:2. = Workbook, Part 1, Lesson 169, Paragraph 5, Sentence 2.

M-13.3:2. = Manual, Question 13, Paragraph 3, Sentence 2.

C-6.4:6 = Clarification of Terms, Term 6, Paragraph 4, Sentence 6.

P-2.VI.5:1. = Psychotherapy, Chapter 2, Section 6, Paragraph 5, Sentence 1.

S-1.V.4:3. = Song of Prayer, Chapter 1, Section 5, Paragraph 4, Sentence 3.

In. = Intro.

YIR. P. 9 = Your Immortal Reality: How to Break the Cycle of Birth and Death by Gary. R. Renard, Page 9

DU. P. 365 = The Disappearance of the Universe by Gary R. Renard, Page 365

ENDNOTES

Foreword. 1. C-1.1:1

1. **Introduction.** 1. T-8.IX.1:5-7 2. T-In.2:2-4 3. W-pI.169.5:1-7 4. T-26.VII.4:7 5. YIR. P.217 6. W-pI.31

2. **What is Health?** 1. T-8.VIII.9:9 2. T-31.I.1:1-3 3. T-8.VIII.1:7-8 4. T-6.V.C.9:7 5. DU. P. 235 6. DU. P. 236 7. DU. P. 80 8. W-pI.5.4:3-4 9. S-1.I.3:6 10. M-4.I.A.3:4

3. **The Purpose of the Body.** 1. T-19.I.3:1-3 2. W-pI.38 3. T-11.V.1:1 4. W-pI.76.5:4 5. T-2.II.1:11-12 6. W-pI.41.1:2-3 7. T-1.VI.2:1 8. T-15.VIII 9. T-31.VIII.9:2 10. W-pI.158.4:5 11. T-10.I.2:1 12. W-pI. 110.3:1

4. **The Power of Choice: Choosing Between Separation or Wholeness.** 1. T-31.VIII.2:3-4 2. T-18.VII.5:7 3. T-18.VII.7:7-8 4. T-18.V.1:6 5. T-11.VIII.2:2-3 6. T-12.VII.8:1 7. T-12.VII.9:1-2 8. W-pI.134.15:3 9. T-14. XI.6:7-9 10. T-18.II.5:12-14 11. T-31.VIII.3:1-2 12. W-pI.185.1:1-2 13. YIR.P.217 14. S-3.III.5:7 15. S-3.II.1:1

16. S-3.II.1:5-6 17. M-20.4:8 18. P-2.VI.1:5-8 19. P-2.
VI.5:5

5. **Empowering Ways to Deal with Pain.** 1.
W-pI.190.3:3-4   2.   T-5.V.5:1   3.   T-31.VIII.5:2-4   4.
W-pI.72.9:2 5. T-18.VII.3:1 6. M-5.II.3:12 7. W-pI.61.5:3
8. M-5.I.1:1-2

6. **Practical Steps to Experience Mental Health.** 1.
M-20.6:1-3 2. T-15.I.9:3 3. S-1.In.1:2 4. S-1.I.2:7-9 5.
S-1.I.3:1-6 6. DU.P.351-352 7. T-30.I.8:2 8. T-30.I.9:2
9. T-30.I.11:4 10. T-30.I.12:3-4 11. W-pI.195.1:5-6 12.
W-pI.195.2:1 13. W-pI.195.6:2-3 14. T-1.III.5:4-6

7. **Change Your Mind, Wake Up to Your Life.** 1.
T-31.VIII.4:1-2 2. T-23.II.19:1-3 3. W-pI.168.3:2 4.
W-pI.135.22:4 5. T-26.V.13:1 6. T-27.VIII.6:2-4 7. T-9.
VII.1:6-7 8. T-6.II.6:1 9. W-pI.188.1:4 10. T-4.in.1:7-8

SUGGESTED READINGS ON *A COURSE IN MIRACLES*

1. "*A Course in Miracles*," 3rd edition, published by the Foundation for Inner Peace

2. "The Disappearance of the Universe" by Gary R. Renard

3. "Your Immortal Reality: How to Break the Cycle of Birth and Death" by Gary R. Renard

4. "Love Has Forgotten No One" by Gary R. Renard

5. "The Most Commonly Asked Questions About A Course in Miracles" by Gloria and Kenneth Wapnick, Ph. D.

6. "Absence From Felicity" by Kenneth Wapnick, Ph.D

7. "Healing the Unhealed Mind" by Kenneth Wapnick, Ph.D

8. "A Vast Illusion" by Kenneth Wapnick, Ph.D

9. "Journey Without Distance" by Robert Skutch

Please see Cindy's website for more information on how to contact her for booking an appearance, a private counseling session as well as ordering from her list of products.

www.cindylora.com

THE FOUNDATION
FOR INNER PEACE

To learn more about *A Course in Miracles*, I recommend you visit the website of the authorized publisher and copyright holder of the Course, the Foundation for Inner Peace: www.acim.org. While there are many excellent organizations supporting study of *A Course in Miracles*, this is the original one with the greatest variety and depth of Course-related materials, including biographies and photos of the scribes, DVDs, free access to daily Lessons, audio recordings, information about the many languages into which the Course has been translated, and electronic versions of the Course, including mobile device apps.

The Foundation for Inner Peace is a non-profit organization dedicated to uplifting humanity through *A Course in Miracles*. The organization depends on donations and is currently immersed in translating the Course into many languages (26 to date). The Foundation also donates thousands of copies of the Course. If you would like to support more people to benefit from *A Course in Miracles*, donating to the Foundation for Inner Peace or one of the many other fine Course-related organizations would be a worthy endeavor.